Paper C05

FUNDAMENTALS OF ETHICS, GOVERNANCE AND BUSINESS LAW

CIMA EXAM PRACTICE KIT

PUBLISHING

WORKING TOGETHER FOR YOU

ELSEVIER

PUBLISHING

CIMA Publishing is an imprint of Elsevier

The Boulevard, Langford Lane, Kidlington, Oxford, OX5 1GB, UK
225 Wyman Street, Waltham, MA02451, USA

Kaplan Publishing UK, Unit 2 The Business Centre, Molly Millars Lane, Wokingham, Berkshire, RG41 2QZ

Notice

No responsibility is assumed by the publisher for any injury and/or damage to persons or property as a matter of products liability, negligence or otherwise, or from any use or operation of any methods, products, instructions or ideas contained in the material herein.

British Library Cataloguing in Publication Data

A catalogue record for this book is available from the British Library

ISBN: 978-0-85732-449-8

Printed and bound in Great Britain.

11 12 13   11 10 9 8 7 6 5 4 3 2 1

CONTENTS

INDEX TO QUESTIONS AND ANSWERS

PRACTICE QUESTIONS

OBJECTIVE TEST QUESTIONS

SYLLABUS GUIDANCE, LEARNING OBJECTIVES AND VERBS

A THE CERTIFICATE IN BUSINESS ACCOUNTING

The Certificate introduces you to management accounting and gives you the basics of accounting and business. There are five subject areas, which are all tested by computer-based assessment (CBA). The five papers are:

- Fundamentals of Management Accounting
- Fundamentals of Financial Accounting
- Fundamentals of Business Mathematics
- Fundamentals of Business Economics
- Fundamentals of Ethics, Corporate Governance and Business Law

The Certificate is both a qualification in its own right and an entry route to the next stage in CIMA's examination structure.

The examination structure after the Certificate comprises:

- Managerial Level
- Strategic Level
- Test of Professional Competence in Management Accounting (an exam based on a case study).

Within each learning pillar there are three syllabus subjects. Two of these subjects are set at the lower "Managerial" level, with the third subject positioned at the higher "Strategic" level. All subject examinations have a duration of three hours and the pass mark is 50 per cent.

Note: In addition to these nine examinations, students are required to gain three years relevant practical experience and successfully sit the Test of Professional Competence in Management Accounting (TOPCIMA).

B AIMS OF THE SYLLABUS

The following are the aims of the syllabus:

- To provide for the Institute, together with the practical experience requirements, an adequate basis for assuring society that those admitted to membership are competent to act as management accountants for entities, whether in manufacturing, commercial or service organisations, in the public or private sectors of the economy;
- To enable the Institute to examine whether prospective members have an adequate knowledge, understanding and mastery of the stated body of knowledge and skills;
- To complement the Institute's practical experience and skills development requirements.

C STUDY WEIGHTINGS

A percentage weighting is shown against each topic in the syllabus. This is intended as a guide to the proportion of study time each topic requires.

All topics in the syllabus must be studied, since any single examination question may examine more than one topic, or carry a higher proportion of marks than the percentage study time suggested.

The weightings do not specify the number of marks that will be allocated to topics in the examination.

D LEARNING OUTCOMES

Each topic within the syllabus contains a list of learning outcomes, which should be read in conjunction with the knowledge content for the syllabus. A learning outcome has two main purposes:

1   to define the skill or ability that a well-prepared candidate should be able to exhibit in the examination;

2   to demonstrate the approach likely to be taken by examiners in examination questions.

The learning outcomes are part of a hierarchy of learning objectives. The verbs used at the beginning of each learning outcome relate to a specific learning objective, e.g. evaluate alternative approaches to budgeting.

The verb "evaluate" indicates a high level learning objective. As learning objectives are hierarchical, it is expected that at this level, students will have knowledge of different budgeting systems and methodologies and be able to apply them.

A list of the learning objectives and the verbs that appear in the syllabus learning outcomes and examinations follows:

Learning objectives	Verbs used	Definition
1 Knowledge		
What you are expected to know	List	Make a list of
	State	Express, fully or clearly, the details of/facts of
	Define	Give the exact meaning of
2 Comprehension		
What you are expected to understand	Describe	Communicate the key features of
	Distinguish	Highlight the differences between
	Explain	Make clear or intelligible/State the meaning of
	Identify	Recognise, establish or select after consideration
	Illustrate	Use an example to describe or explain something

3	Application		
	How you are expected to apply your knowledge	Apply	To put to practical use
		Calculate/compute	To ascertain or reckon mathematically
		Demonstrate	To prove with certainty or to exhibit by practical means
		Prepare	To make or get ready for use
		Reconcile	To make or prove consistent/compatible
		Solve	Find an answer to
		Tabulate	Arrange in a table
4	Analysis		
	How you are expected to analyse the detail of what you have learned	Analyse	Examine in detail the structure of
		Categorise	Place into a defined class or division
		Compare and contrast	Show the similarities and/or differences between
		Construct	To build up or compile
		Discuss	To examine in detail by argument
		Interpret	To translate into intelligible or familiar terms
		Produce	To create or bring into existence
5	Evaluation	Evaluation	
	How you are expected to use your learning to evaluate, make decisions or recommendations	Advise	To counsel, inform or notify
		Evaluate	To appraise or assess the value of
		Recommend	To advise on a course of action

E COMPUTER-BASED ASSESSMENT

CIMA has introduced computer-based assessment (CBA) for all subjects at Certificate level. CIMA uses objective test questions in the computer-based assessment. The most common types are:

- multiple choice, where you have to choose the correct answer from a list of four possible answers. This could either be numbers or text.

- multiple choice with more choices and answers – for example, choosing two correct answers from a list of eight possible answers. This could either be numbers or text.

- single numeric entry, where you give your numeric answer e.g. profit is $10,000.

- multiple entry, where you give several numeric answers e.g. the charge for electricity is $2000 and the accrual is $200.

- true/false questions, where you state whether a statement is true or false e.g. external auditors report to the directors is FALSE.
- matching pairs of text e.g. the convention 'prudence' would be matched with the statement' inventories revalued at the lower of cost and net realisable value'.
- other types could be matching text with graphs and labelling graphs/diagrams.

In this Exam Practice Kit we have used these types of questions.

For further CBA practice, CIMA Publishing has produced CIMA eSuccess CD-ROMs for all certificate level subjects. These will be available from www.cimapublishing.com

F FUNDAMENTALS OF ETHICS, CORPORATE GOVERNANCE AND BUSINESS LAW

The examination is a 2-hour computer-based assessment (CBA) comprising 75 compulsory questions, with one or more parts. Single part questions are generally worth 1-2 marks each, but two and three part questions may be worth 4 or 6 marks. There will be no choice and all questions should be attempted if time permits. CIMA are continuously developing the question styles within the CBA system and you are advised to try the on-line website demo at www.cimaglobal.com, to both gain familiarity with assessment software and examine the latest style of questions being used. CIMA Publishing have also produced testing CD's which will be available from www.cimapublishing.com.

G SYLLABUS OUTLINE

Syllabus overview

The learning outcomes in this paper reflect the legal framework for business and provide the underpinning for commercial activity. It includes the areas of contract law, employment law, financing, administration and management of companies. The globalisation of business is recognised by the inclusion of alternative legal systems, as well as the English legal system. Judicial precedent is included in relation to professional negligence.

Wherever business is conducted, the highest professional standards must be demonstrated for the benefit of all stakeholders. With this in mind, the place of ethics and ethical conflict is considered, as well as the role of corporate governance and its increasing impact in the management of organisations.

Syllabus structure

The syllabus comprises the following topics and study weightings:

A	Ethics and business	15%
B	Ethical conflict	10%
C	Corporate governance	10%
D	Comparison of English law with alternative legal systems	10%
E	The law of contract	20%
F	The law of employment	10%
G	Company administration and finance	25%

Assessment strategy

There will be a two hour computer based assessment, comprising 75 compulsory questions, each with one or more parts.

A variety of objective test question styles and types will be used within the assessment.

C05 – A. Ethics and business (15%)

Learning outcomes
On completion of their studies students should be able to:

Lead	Component		Level	Indicative syllabus content
1 demonstrate an understanding of the importance of ethics to business generally and to the professional accountant.	(a)	apply the values and attitudes that provide professional accountants with a commitment to act in the public interest and with social responsibility;	3	• The importance of ethics. • Values and attitudes for professional accountants.
	(b)	explain the need for a framework of laws, regulations and standards in business and their application;	2	• Legal frameworks, regulations and standards for business. • The role of national 'Professional Oversight Boards for Accountancy' and 'Auditing Practices Boards'. • The role of international accounting bodies e.g. IFAC.
	(c)	explain the nature of ethics and its application to business and the accountancy profession;	2	• The nature of ethics and its relevance to business and the accountancy profession.
	(d)	distinguish between detailed rules-based and framework approaches to ethics.	2	• Rules based and framework approaches to ethics. • The 'Seven Principles of Public Life' – selflessness, integrity, objectivity, accountability, openness, honesty and leadership.
2 explain the need for CIMA members to adopt the highest standards of ethical behaviour.	(a)	explain the need for continual personal improvement and life-long learning;	2	• Personal development and lifelong learning. • The personal qualities of reliability, responsibility, timeliness, courtesy and respect.
	(b)	explain the need to develop the virtues of reliability, responsibility, timeliness, courtesy and respect;	2	
	(c)	explain the ethical principles of integrity, objectivity, professional competence, due care and confidentiality;	2	• The ethical principles of integrity and objectivity. • Professional competence, due care and confidentiality.
	(d)	identify concepts of independence, scepticism, accountability and social responsibility;	2	• Disclosure required by law. • The concepts of independence, scepticism, accountability and social responsibility.
	(e)	explain the reasons why CIMA and IFAC each have a 'Code of Ethics for Professional Accountants'.	2	• The CIMA and IFAC 'Code of Ethics for Professional Accountants'.

C05 – B. Ethical conflict (10%)

Learning outcomes

On completion of their studies students should be able to:

Lead	Component		Level	Indicative syllabus content
1 explain the various means of regulating ethical behaviour.	(a)	explain the relationship between ethics, governance, the law and social responsibility;	2	• The relationship between ethics and the law. • The distinction between ethical codes and contracts. • Corporate governance and social responsibility. • Unethical behaviour. • The consequences of unethical behaviour.
	(b)	describe the consequences of unethical behaviour to the individual, the profession and society.	2	
2 explain how ethical dilemmas and conflicts of interest arise and may be resolved.	(a)	identify situations where ethical dilemmas and conflicts of interest occur;	2	• The nature of ethical dilemmas. • Conflicts of interest and how they arise. • Ethical conflict resolution. • The CIMA Code of Ethics for Professional Accountants – 'Fundamental Principles'.
	(b)	explain how ethical dilemmas and conflicts of interest can be resolved.	2	

C05 – C. Corporate governance (10%)

Learning outcomes

On completion of their studies students should be able to:

Lead	Component		Level	Indicative syllabus content
1 explain the development of corporate governance to meet public concern in relation to the management of companies.	(a)	define corporate governance;	1	• The role and key objectives of corporate governance. • The interaction of corporate governance, ethics and the law. • The development of corporate governance internationally e.g. in the UK, Europe, South Africa and the USA. • Rules and principles based approaches to governance.
	(b)	explain the interaction of corporate governance with business ethics and company law;	2	
	(c)	describe the history of corporate governance internationally;	2	
	(d)	distinguish between detailed rules-based and principles based approaches to governance.	2	

Lead	Component		Level	Indicative syllabus content
2 explain the impact of corporate governance on the directors and management structure of public limited companies and how this benefits stakeholders.	(a)	explain the effects of corporate governance on directors' powers and duties;	2	• The impact of corporate governance on directors' powers and duties.
	(b)	describe different board structures, the role of the board and corporate social responsibility;	2	• Types of board structures, the role of the board and corporate social responsibility (CSR).
	(c)	describe the types of policies and procedures that constitute 'best practice';	2	• The role of the board in establishing corporate governance standards. • Corporate governance codes e.g. The UK Corporate Governance Code. • Policies and procedures for 'best practice' companies.
	(d)	explain the regulatory governance framework for companies and benefits to stakeholders.	2	• The regulatory governance framework for companies. • Stakeholder benefits.

C05 - D. Comparison of English law with alternative legal systems (10%)

Learning outcomes
On completion of their studies students should be able to:

Lead	Component		Level	Indicative syllabus content
1 explain the essential elements of the English legal system and the tort of negligence.	(a)	explain the manner in which behaviour within society is regulated by the civil and the criminal law;	2	• The purpose of civil and criminal law. • The sources of English law: custom, case law, statute, European law and other sources.
	(b)	explain the sources of English law;	2	• The distinction between the common law and equity.
	(c)	illustrate the operation of the doctrine of precedent by reference to the essential elements of the tort of negligence and its application to professional advisers;	2	• The system of judicial precedent. • The essential elements of the tort of negligence, including duty, breach and damage/loss/injury and the liability of professionals in respect of negligent advice.

Lead	Component		Level	Indicative syllabus content
2 describe the essential elements of alternative legal systems	(a)	describe the characteristics of the legal systems found in other countries;	2	• Alternative legal systems, including codified (civil law) systems. • The general characteristics of the legal systems of France, Germany, Poland, Italy, Denmark, Greece and Cyprus. • The general characteristics of the legal systems of the USA, Malaysia, China and Sri Lanka. • Elements of Shari'ah Law including sources of Shari'ah law and the Five Pillars of Islam. • The benefits of international regulations for commerce and professional practice through the work of key bodies e.g. IFAC, ISO, FEE.
	(b)	describe elements of Shari'ah law;	2	
	(c)	describe the role of international regulations.	2	

C05 – E. The law of contract (20%)

Learning outcomes

On completion of their studies students should be able to:

Lead	Component		Level	Indicative syllabus content
1 explain how the law determines the point at which a contract is formed and the legal status of contractual terms.	(a)	identify the essential elements of a valid simple contract and situations where the law requires the contract to be in a particular form;	2	• The essential elements of a valid simple contract.
	(b)	explain how the law determines whether negotiating parties have reached agreement and the role of consideration in making that agreement enforceable;	2	• The legal status of statements made by negotiating parties. Offers and acceptances and the application of the rules to standard form contracts using modern forms of communication.
	(c)	explain when the parties will be regarded as intending the agreement to be legally binding and how an agreement may be avoided because of misrepresentations;	2	• The principles for establishing that the parties intend their agreement to have contractual force and how a contract is affected by a misrepresentation.
	(d)	explain how the terms of a contract are established and their status determined;	2	• Incorporation of express and implied terms, conditions and warranties
	(e)	describe the effect of terms implied into contracts by sale of goods and supply of goods and services legislation;	2	• The main provisions of the Sale of Goods Act 1979 and the Supply of Goods and Services Act 1982.
	(f)	describe how the law controls the use of excluding, limiting and unfair terms.	2	• Excluding and limiting terms; the Unfair Contract Terms Act 1977 and the Unfair Terms in Consumer Contracts Regulations.

Lead		Component	Level	Indicative syllabus content
2	explain when the law regards a contract as discharged and the remedies available for breach and non-performance.	(a) describe the factors which cause a contract to be discharged;	2	• Discharge of a contract by performance, agreement and breach.
		(b) explain how the law of frustration provides an excuse for non-performance of the contract;	2	• The law relating to frustration. • The law relating to damages.
		(c) explain the remedies which are available for serious and minor breaches of contract.	2	• The remedies of specific performance, injunction, rescission, and requiring a contract party to pay the agreed price.

C05 – F. The law of employment (10%)

Learning outcomes
On completion of their studies students should be able to:

Lead		Component	Level	Indicative syllabus content
1	explain the essential elements of an employment contract and the remedies available following termination of the contract.	(a) explain the differences between employees and independent contractors;	2	• The tests used to distinguish an employee from an independent contractor.
		(b) explain how the contents of a contract of employment are established;	2	• The express and implied terms of a contract of employment.
		(c) explain the distinction between unfair and wrongful dismissal.	2	• The rights and duties of employers and employees. • Notice and dismissal. • Unfair and wrongful dismissal.
2	explain the impact of health and safety law on employers and employees.	(a) explain how employers and employees are affected by health and safety legislation;	2	• The main rules relating to health and safety at work, sanctions on employers for non-compliance, and remedies for employees.
		(b) describe the consequences of a failure to comply with health and safety legislation.	2	• Social security compensation. • Civil liability for occupational injuries.

C05 – G. Company administration and finance (25%)

Learning outcomes

On completion of their studies students should be able to:

Lead		Component	Level	Indicative syllabus content
1 explain the nature, legal status and administration of business organisations.	(a)	describe the essential characteristics of the different forms of business organisations and the implications of corporate personality;	2	• The essential characteristics of sole traderships/practitionerships, partnerships, companies limited by shares and corporate personality.
	(b)	explain the differences between public and private companies and establishing a company by registration or purchasing 'off the shelf';	2	• 'Lifting the corporate veil' both at common law and by statute.
	(c)	explain the purpose and legal status of the articles of association;	2	• The distinction between public and private companies.
	(d)	explain the ability of a company to contract;	2	• Company registration and the advantages of purchasing a company 'off the shelf'.
	(e)	explain the main advantages and disadvantages of carrying on business through the medium of a company limited by shares;	2	• The purpose and contents of the articles of association.
	(f)	explain the use and procedure of board meetings and general meetings of shareholders;	2	• Corporate capacity to contract.
	(g)	explain the voting rights of directors and shareholders;	2	• The advantages and disadvantages of the company limited by shares.
	(h)	identify the various types of shareholder resolutions.		• Board meetings: when used and the procedure at the meeting.
				• General Meetings of shareholders: when used and the procedure at the meeting.
				• The voting rights of directors and shareholders.
				• Ordinary, special and written resolutions and their uses.

2 explain the law relating to the financing and management of companies limited by shares.			
	(a)	explain the nature of different types of shares, the procedure for their issue and acceptable forms of payment;	2
	(b)	explain the maintenance of capital principle and the reduction of share capital;	2
	(c)	explain the ability of a company to take secured and unsecured loans, the different types of security and the registration procedure;	2
	(d)	explain the procedure for the appointment, retirement, disqualification and removal of directors;	2
	(e)	explain the powers and duties of directors when in office;	2
	(f)	explain the rules dealing with the possible imposition of personal liability upon the directors of insolvent companies;	2
	(g)	explain the rights of majority and minority shareholders;	2
	(h)	explain the division of powers between the board of a company and the shareholders;	2
	(i)	explain the qualifications, powers and duties of the company secretary.	2

Indicative syllabus content:

- The rights attaching to different types of shares.
- The procedures for issuing shares.
- The issue of shares for an improper purpose. Payment for shares.
- The maintenance of capital principle: the purposes for which shares may be issued, redeemed or, purchased and the provision of financial assistance for the purchase of the company's own shares.
- The reduction of capital.
- The ability of a company to borrow money and the procedure to be followed.
- Unsecured loans, and the nature and effect of fixed and floating charges.
- The appointment, retirement and removal of directors and their powers and duties during office.
- Fraudulent and wrongful trading, preferences and transactions at an under-value.
- The rights of majority and minority shareholders.
- The division of powers between the board and the shareholders.
- The qualifications, powers and duties of the company secretary.

EXAMINATION TECHNIQUES

COMPUTER-BASED EXAMINATIONS

TEN GOLDEN RULES

1 Make sure you are familiar with the software before you start the exam. You cannot speak to the invigilator once you have started.

2 These exam practice kits give you plenty of exam style questions to practice.

3 Attempt all questions, there is no negative marking.

4 Double check your answer before you put in the final answer.

5 On multiple choice questions (MCQs) there is only one correct answer.

6 Not all questions will be MCQs – you may have to fill in missing words or figures.

7 Identify the easy questions first and get some points on the board to build up your confidence.

8 Try and allow 15 minutes at the end to check your answers and make any corrections.

9 If you don't know the answer, try a process of elimination.

10 Take scrap paper, pen and calculator with you. Work out your answer on paper first if it is easier for you.

Section 1

PRACTICE QUESTIONS

COMPARISON OF ENGLISH LAW WITH ALTERNATIVE LEGAL SYSTEMS

Comparison of Criminal and Civil Law

(a)	Purpose	Criminal – regulation of society through the threat of punishment
		Civil – compensation of the victim
(b)	Case brought by	Criminal – the state
		Civil – the victim
(c)	Action	Criminal – prosecution
		Civil – suing
(d)	Burden of proof	Criminal – beyond reasonable doubt
		Civil – on a balance of probabilities
(e)	Court	Criminal – Magistrate's Court, Crown Court
		Civil – County Court, High Court
(f)	Outcome if defendant loses	Criminal – imprisonment, fine, community service, probation
		Civil – damages, specific performance, injunction

JUDICIAL PRECEDENT

Sources of law

There are two main sources of law in the UK.

1   Acts of Parliament (sometimes called statutes).

2   Case Law developed by the courts.

The meaning of judicial precedent

When a Judge decides a case before him, his judgment will have to be based on some legal principle or process of legal reasoning. It is desirable that in all the future cases of a similar kind the same process of legal reasoning should apply.

Case Law is based on two fundamental principles.

1   The doctrine of binding precedent.

2   The hierarchy of the Courts.

A Judge is bound to apply the rules of law contained in earlier decisions of a higher Court and usually those of a Court of equal standing.

Not everything said is binding in later cases. We have to distinguish between *ratio decidendi* – the legal principle on which the Judge bases his decision – and *obiter dicta* – other remarks made in passing.

Ratio decidendi

The only thing that binds the Judge in a later case is the *ratio decidendi*, that is the legal reasoning for the decision. It is important to note that the *ratio* has nothing to do with the specific facts of the case; it is a general statement of law which is applicable to those material facts (and will be applicable to future cases where the facts are similar).

Obiter dicta

Not every statement of Law in a judgment is binding. Only statements based on facts found in that particular case and on which the decision is based form the *ratio* of the case. All other statements are merely comments of the Judge, which are called *obiter dicta* (things said by the way or in passing).

THE HIERARCHY OF THE COURTS

The *ratio* of a case establishes a precedent and must be applied in any similar case unless and until it is overruled by a higher Court than the one which first formulated it or by Act of Parliament.

The House of Lords (Supreme Court)

From the 5th October 2009 the House of Lords as the senior domestic court became the Supreme Court. This is the highest Court in England and Wales and its decisions are binding on all lower Courts. Since 1966 the House is no longer bound by its own previous decisions and will depart from its previous *ratio* where the Lords consider it would lead to injustice or would restrict the development of Law.

The Court of Appeal

The Court of Appeal's decisions are binding on all Courts except the House of Lords (Supreme Court), but it is bound by its own previous decisions.

The High Court of Justice

A single High Court Judge is bound by the decisions of higher Courts (i.e. the House of Lords (Supreme Court) and the Court of Appeal) but is not bound by the decisions of another High Court Judge.

Lower Courts

Lower Courts (i.e. Crown, County and Magistrate's Courts) are all bound by decisions of higher Courts.

Exceptions to the doctrine of judicial precedent

A Judge must follow the legal principles pronounced by his predecessors. There are exceptions to this rule.

(a)   The precedent may have been overruled subsequently, either by statute (i.e. a subsequent Act of Parliament) or by a higher Court (e.g. where the House of Lords (Supreme Court) overrules an earlier decision of the Court of Appeal).

(b)   The original decision may have been made through lack of care by a previous Judge. Later Judges are not bound to follow an earlier Judge who was clearly in error (*per incuriam*).

(c)   The later case may be distinguished on its facts, that is the facts of the case are different in a material respect from those of the previous case.

(d)   The ratio may be obscured and so cannot clearly be identified. This may occur when a conclusion in a case is reached by more than one Judge, each giving a different reason for his conclusion. (In the House of Lords (Supreme Court) five Judges will sit, each giving an individual judgment.)

Advantages of judicial precedent

Certainty – ensuring that people can assess their chances of success without wasting time or money.

Reform and flexibility – precedents can be modified and developed to meet the changing needs of society.

A great wealth of detailed rules – cases have been reported for centuries, therefore Judges are guided when making decisions.

Disadvantages of judicial precedent

The danger of illogical decisions – the system encourages a Judge to make artificial distinctions between the cases in order to avoid following precedent.

Rigidity – the binding force of precedent is a restraint on the discretion of the Judge which may lead to an unfair result.

Bulk and complexity of the system – the number of reported cases is so vast that Law can be ascertained only by searching through a large number of reports.

Judge-made law – decisions are made by Judges who are not democratically elected.

Retrospective character – it is retrospective in nature as it is only formulated as the need arises.

The tort of negligence

A tort is a civil wrong, for example negligence, nuisance, trespass or defamation.

A tort arises independently of a contract, the basic remedy for a breach being a claim for unliquidated damages.

The person who commits the tort is known as the 'Tortfeasor' and he will always be liable.

Negligence

For a plaintiff to be successful in his claim the following essential elements must be present:

(a)   The defendant owed him a duty of care;

(b)   The defendant breached that duty;

(c)   As a result the plaintiff suffered damage.

Duty of care

People owe a duty to their neighbours to take reasonable care to avoid negligent acts or omissions (*Donoghue v Stevenson* 1932).

The duty of care is owed not only to the primary victim but also to secondary victims for nervous shock.

Statute also imposes a duty of care to occupiers of premises under the Occupiers Liability Act 1957 (visitors) and the Occupiers Liabilities Act 1984 (trespassers).

Breach of duty

As a general rule, the plaintiff must show that the defendant failed to take reasonable care. Professional person's standards are higher dependant on the standard and practices at the time. Amateurs undertaking skilled work will have to reach the standard of a competent worker.

Res Ipsa Loquitur

This means the 'facts speak for themselves'. Generally the plaintiff must prove that he was owed a duty and it was breached. Res Ipsa Loquitur reverses the burden of proof to the defendant to rebut negligence (*Mahon v Osbourne* 1939).

Resultant damage

The defendant's act must be the principal cause of the plaintiff's loss, that is the 'But for' test. If the plaintiff would have suffered damage regardless of the defendant's actions, no liability will arise.

Novus actus interveniens

This is where a new act intervenes to break the chain of causation between the defendant's wrongful act and the subsequent damage sustained by the plaintiff.

Negligent misstatement

Professional persons, for example solicitors and accountants, can be sued for breach of contract should a contractual relationship exist. They can also be sued for negligent statements that are made to third parties.

The basic tests for negligence must be shown – Duty, Breach and Damage.

Liability is owed for the consequences of negligent statements causing pure financial loss where the parties have a special relationship.

A special relationship will exist where a person makes a statement in an expert or professional capacity and he knows that others may reasonably rely upon it without taking any further advice.

These principles were established in *Hedley Byrne v Heller and Partners* 1963 and developed in *Caparo Industries plc v Dickman* 1990.

The current position regarding accountants and auditors is that liability will be owed to the recipient where advice has been:

(a)   Communicated directly or indirectly;

(b)   Used for the specific purpose given;

(c)   Relied upon by the plaintiff.

The Floodgate test applies here, that is that the giver of the information will be liable only when it would be reasonable to do so in the public interest.

Consequently, accountants and auditors owe a duty to the Company as a whole, that is the shareholders as a corporate body, not to individual shareholders unless specific assurances were given.

OTHER ISSUES

Vicarious liability

The person who commits the tort, the tortfeasor, is always liable but another may be held vicariously liable having joint and several liability. This is the situation in an employer-employee relationship.

The employer will be liable where the employee commits a tort 'within the course of his employment'.

The employer will not be liable where the employee is acting outside the course of employment.

The principle has no general application to Independent Contractors.

Contributory negligence

The Law Reform (contributory negligence) Act 1943 allows the courts to reduce damages proportionately to the extent a plaintiff has contributed to his own injuries (*Sayers v Harlow UDC 1958*).

Volenti non fit injuria

Meaning – no injury can be done to a willing person and thus the defendant is not liable.

Volenti equals consent. Consent may be express or implied knowledge of the possibility of harm.

Employees rarely consent voluntarily to the risk of harm. Rescuers or persons acting in an emergency situation also do not consent to potential harm.

Exclusion clauses

The Unfair Contract Terms Act 1977 prohibits the use by businesses of clauses excluding death or personal injury if caused by their negligence. Such a provision would be void.

Any other exclusion, that is for financial loss, would be void unless shown to be reasonable.

The common law

The common law has gradually developed since the Norman Conquest in 1066. By the 12th century, commissioners were being used for legal as well as fiscal and administrative purposes and were referred to as itinerant justices. The itinerants all came from a central source, the justice which they administered also became unified and developed into a law which was common throughout the country, the common law.

The writ system

The injured party in a case would issue a writ against the other party. When an itinerant justice next appeared, the writ would be heard in court and the matter decided.

Parliament, another newly emerging body, regarded the invention of new writs as a usurpation of its powers as the supreme lawgiver and, in 1258, the Provisions of Oxford forbade the practice of creating new writs.

The development of equity

There were a number of problems with the common law.

(a)   It was too rigid, owing to the inability to issue new writs and thereby recognise new problems. Cases had to be fitted into an existing definition.

(b)   It was entangled in procedure, making justice slow and expensive to obtain.

(c)   The only real remedy available was damages, which was not appropriate in every case.

As a result, people who felt they had an unsatisfactory outcome began to petition the King directly. The King delegated the task of hearing such appeals to the Lord Chancellor. In this way an additional branch of law, known as 'equity' developed.

Under the new system of equity, cases were decided not exclusively on the basis of what had gone before but on the basis of fairness, justice and morality.

Equity initially concentrated on:

(a)   new rights and the solution to new problems originally not recognised by the common law; and

(b)   on the development of remedies, the purpose of which was to counter the inefficiency of injustice of common law.

Its main features were as follows:

(a)   fairness;

(b)   flexibility;

(c)   additional remedies (injunctions and decrees of specific performance).

Equity did not replace the common law. The common law courts often produced a satisfactory conclusion and no recourse to equity was required. Equity was therefore 'a gloss on the common law', not a substitute for it.

In cases of conflict between the two, however, equity prevailed.

Equitable principles and remedies are discretionary. Common law remedies are available as of right.

Equity developed non–monetary remedies which include injunctions and specific performance orders. The former serves to prohibit conduct, whilst the latter is a court order compelling a party to act in a specified way.

STATUTES AND THEIR INTERPRETATION

Legislation

In its widest sense the term 'legislation' includes all methods of making law. To legislate is to make new law in any fashion.

In its narrow or strict sense, legislation is that source of law which consists of the declaration of legal rules by a competent authority. In the UK, legislation is made by Parliament.

Legislation may be used to develop law by:

(a)   enacting new law;

(b)   repealing old law or altering it;

(c)   consolidating existing statutes, for example Companies Act 2006;

(d)   codifying existing law of all sources which means to bring together law from various sources including decisions of cases and put them into statute.

Law created by legislation is generally referred to as statute.

Forms of legislation

Supreme legislation

This legislation proceeds from the supreme or sovereign power in the state and therefore cannot be repealed, annulled or controlled by any other legislative authority. In England, supreme legislative authority is vested in Parliament and is expressed in the form of Acts of Parliament.

Subordinate legislation

Parliament delegates some legislative powers to e.g. ministers, government departments and local authorities. Such delegated legislation must remain within the power conferred by Parliament and may be questioned in the courts on the grounds that it exceeds these limits (i.e. it is ultra *vires*).

The legislative process

A statute is law that has been passed by the House of Commons and the House of Lords and has received Royal Assent. Not all legislation is created through the normal process. For example, the Finance Act that follows the budget is a clear exception.

The procedure involved is as follows:

First reading

This is purely formal. The title of the bill and the name of the member introducing it is read out by an official and the bill is then ordered to be printed.

Second reading

This involves a discussion of the general principles of the bill. If nobody opposes it or if a vote is taken on the bill and there is a majority in favour of it, the bill will pass on to the committee stage.

Committee stage

At this stage the bill is examined in detail by a committee made up in the same proportions as the House of Commons.

Report stage

At the report stage, the committee which has considered the bill will report back to the House on its discussion and proposed amendments.

Third reading

This constitutes the final debate on the general principles of the bill and a vote is taken. Assuming the bill passes its third reading, it then passes to the other House.

The House of Lords

The procedure followed in the Commons is repeated in the Lords.

The Royal Assent

After a bill has passed through both Houses of Parliament, it receives the Royal Assent and unless the bill provides anything to the contrary it will immediately become law.

Statutory interpretation

Judges have a number of rules, aids and presumptions that can assist them when interpreting legislation.

The literal rule – where wording has only one meaning, that meaning should be adopted even though it results in an absurd decision.

The golden rule – where wording has more than one meaning, the meaning that avoids an absurd result should be adopted.

The mischief rule – where parliament has introduced legislation in order to remedy a mischief in the law, the legislation should be interpreted to achieve this objective.

The purposive approach – a modern version of the mischief rule. Parliaments purpose in introducing the legislation should be considered on interpretation of wording.

The Rules of language

Ejusdem generis – the meaning of general wording is to be taken from the meaning of specific wording used.

Expressio unius est exclusio alterius – where wording is specific, then that omitted is deemed to be excluded.

Noscitur a sociis – other words found in the legislation serve to enable the meaning of other wording to be determined.

In pari material – previous legislation serves to assist in providing meanings.

Delegated legislation

This is the procedure whereby Parliament delegates the ability to legislate to ministers or government departments.

Forms of delegated legislation include the following:

(a)   *Orders in council.* These are enacted under powers delegated to the Privy Council (i.e. the Cabinet).

(b)   *Ministerial regulations.* These are known as statutory instruments which are made by individual ministers within some limited sphere relating to their departmental responsibilities, for example interest rates on late payment of tax.

(c)   *Bye-laws.* Local authorities are given powers by many Acts of Parliament to make bye-laws operative within their own geographical areas, for example on park opening hours and parking regulations.

Advantages of delegated legislation

(a)   It relieves pressure upon parliamentary time.

(b)   Delegated legislation enables rapid changes to be made in the law.

(c)   Subordinate legislation is more flexible than supreme legislation, which can only be changed by more legislation.

(d)   As regards legislation on technical topics, delegated legislation enables legislators to consult with experts and interests concerned.

The main disadvantage of delegated legislation is that it is made by a body which is arguably not truly representative of and accountable to the people.

Control of delegated legislation

Just as parliament provides the power for the creation of delegated legislation, so also it can create new legislation to take away or vary this power. Parliament has a supervisory role over the introduction of delegated legislation, and a Scrutiny Committee exists to serve as a control. Because of the volume of delegated legislation introduced, the effectiveness of parliamentary controls can be questioned.

The Judiciary can also act to control delegated legislation where a body has acted ultra vires (beyond the power it has been given).

EUROPEAN LAW

Efforts are made to remove differences between member states' rules governing trade and commerce so that economic activity may be pursued just as easily in one member state as another.

The Single European Act, implemented from 1 January 1993, seeks to create a truly 'common' market by allowing for free movement of goods, services, people and capital.

Sources of European law

The European Union is governed by its own law, the sources of which are as follows:

(a)   Treaties made between the member states. The most important is the Treaty establishing the European Economic Community (known as the EEC Treaty) which was made in 1957;

(b)   Regulations made by the Commission;

(c)   The case law of the European Court of Justice, which is also known as the Court of Justice of the European Communities (CJEC);

(d)   Directives adopted by the Council.

The council consists of one member from the government of every member state and is commonly called the 'Council of Ministers'. The Council makes decisions only by unanimous agreement so that in principle no member state should have a decision imposed on it by the opinion of a majority of members.

In each member state, Community law has effect as if it were part of the member's internal law. Parliament made Community law a part of UK law by enacting the European Communities Act 1972, s2(1).

Conflict between EU and national law

It is possible for European Union law to be in conflict with the national law of a member state. For example, national law may require payment of a customs duty that has been prohibited by European Union law. The CJEC has repeatedly said that European Union law must be given precedence in such a case. In practice, the governments of member states have always acted to remove inconsistencies between national and European Union law, though sometimes with reluctance.

THE EUROPEAN UNION AND DOMESTIC LEGAL SYSTEMS

The European Union at present is made up of 27 states. A codified system of law is to be found in a significant number of these states. In France a Code Civile was created and today the law is mainly created by the legislature and so retains the codified nature of the law. Germany also has a codified system with law created by Parliament and found in codified acts. The judiciary are also required to follow customary law and must also interpret codified law in reaching judgments. Poland and Italy are democratic republics and each have a parliament with the power of creating legislation. In both of these countries the creation of legislation is subject to the content of the countries' Constitution. Whilst the procedure for statute creation, court structure and recognition of other sources of law found in the states of the European Union are in many instances similar to that found in the UK, a codified system of law in the formal sense does not exist in the UK.

Legal systems around the world have developed from often adopting the law established elsewhere as its base. Roman Law and English Law have provided this foundation for legal development in a number of countries. Malaysia has a legal system based on the English Common Law. Likewise in Sri Lanka, British Laws were originally applied. Hong Kong and Macau similarly adopted English Law and following the transfer of sovereignty to China, continue to adopt the English Common Law, but also have a Portuguese influence. The role of governments, the existence of a Constitution and the court structures found in countries around the world often are very similar. Differences in the level of development of legal systems can be found. Whilst Roman Law and English Law are long established, countries such as China have made progress towards establishing a legal system, but further development is still needed in order to have a system that can be likened to that found in many other countries.

SHARIA LAW

Sharia Law can be recognised as divided into two parts. The first part relates to religion and worship, the second part relating to court process and the judiciary. Included also are family law matters, commercial law and punishments applicable.

Features of Sharia Law include Freedom of Speech, Muslim apostates where apostasy is likened to the crime of treason, dietary laws and the role of women.

The following are the primary sources of Sharia Law:

1   The Qur'an.

2   The Sunnah (the Way) recognising directions of the Prophet Muhammad and on some issues the disciples of Muhammad.

Secondary sources are found through reasoning where no rules exist, and consensus of the people.

The interpretation of Sharia Law differs in different societies, likewise rules relating to court procedures, evidence and the burden of proof can be seen to differ in countries where Sharia Law is applied.

INTERNATIONAL LEGAL REGULATIONS

International law has developed which relates to the dealings between nations. Public International Law relates to dealings between states and the subjects of states. Private International Law relates to issues involving individuals where the issue relates to more than one state. Where an inconsistency is found in the pursuance of practices by states, international law will emerge. International agreements which are binding on the relevant states can take whatever form the relevant parties wish. The primary sources of International Law are customs and conventions.

Just as states can enter into agreements, so organisations can enter into agreements that are binding on an international scale. Collective agreements within defined areas of the world can also emerge.

THE ENGLISH LEGAL SYSTEM AND THE STRUCTURE OF THE COURTS

The criminal courts of England and Wales

The Magistrate's Court

Personnel

These courts are usually staffed by lay persons (also called Justices of the Peace) who are appointed by the Lord Chancellor. Each bench of magistrates is assisted by a salaried clerk who is legally qualified and advises them on law and procedure. Some Magistrate's courts, especially those in larger cities are staffed by professional magistrates known as District Judges.

Jurisdiction

In criminal proceedings the magistrates deal with three main types of offences.

1   *Summary offences.* These are only triable by the Magistrate's Court – not assisted by a jury; the maximum penalty that can be imposed by magistrates is six months imprisonment and/or a fine of up to £5,000.

2   *Offences triable by either the Magistrate's Court or the Crown Court.* These offences are known as offences triable either way, depending on how serious these offences are. There is a preliminary hearing in the Magistrate's Court. If it is considered serious, the matter will be referred to the Crown Court. The accused has the right to demand for this type of offence to have a trial by jury in the Crown Court. If the offence is tried by the Magistrates Court and the accused is found guilty, the magistrates may still commit him for sentence to the Crown Court as their penalty is still limited.

3   *Indictable offences.* These are triable by the Crown Court. The most serious criminal offences (e.g. murder, rape) must be tried on indictment in the Crown Court. The magistrates hold a preliminary investigation known as committal proceedings to ensure that the prosecution have sufficient evidence to warrant a trial.

Appeals procedure

Only the defendant may appeal from the Magistrate's Court to the Crown Court on the grounds of sentence and/or conviction on questions of law and fact.

The Crown Court

Personnel

There are three types of Judge who may sit in this court: a High Court Judge, a Circuit Judge and a part-time Judge known as a Recorder.

Jurisdiction

The Crown Court deals with the most serious criminal offences (e.g. murder, manslaughter, treason, robbery, etc.). It has an appellate jurisdiction, hearing appeals by the accused on law, fact and sentence from the Magistrate's Court.

Appeals procedure

An appeal would lie to the Court of Appeal Criminal Division by the accused on points of law, law and fact, or against sentence. There is also an appeal to the Divisional Court of the Queen's Bench on a point of law by either prosecution or defence by way of case stated.

The Court of Appeal Criminal Division

Personnel

The head of the court is the Lord Chief Justice and he is assisted by Lords Justices of Appeal. To hear a case, usually three of these will sit.

Jurisdiction

The court hears appeals by the accused from the Crown Court on sentence, conviction, questions of law and fact. The court can quash a conviction, reduce a sentence or, in some cases, order a new trial.

Appeals procedure

An appeal lies to the House of Lords. However, a point of law of general public importance must be involved and either the Appeal Court itself or the House of Lords must grant permission for the point to be considered by the House.

The House of Lords (The Supreme Court)

Personnel

The head of the court is the Lord Chancellor who is assisted by Lords of Appeal in Ordinary (the Law Lords). When an appeal is heard, a minimum of three of these Judges will sit but if the case is of fundamental importance five judges will sit.

Jurisdiction

The House of Lords hears appeals from the Court of Appeal Criminal Division and the Divisional Court of the Queen's Bench. All appeals are on points of law by prosecution or defence.

THE CIVIL COURTS IN ENGLAND AND WALES

The Magistrate's Court

Jurisdiction

The civil jurisdiction of magistrates is fairly small. However, they do exercise authority in the following areas:

(a)   The Children's Act 1989.

(b)   Affiliation cases.

(c)   Guardianship and adoption proceedings.

(d)   Actions for unpaid council tax and business rates.

(e)   Licensing of betting offices and liquor licenses.

Appeals procedure

Appeal from the decision of magistrates in family matters (items a-c) lies to the Divisional Court of the Family Division and under item e to the Crown Court.

County Courts

Personnel

A county court is staffed by Circuit Judges and District Judges.

Jurisdiction

Matters involving Contract and Tort (civil wrongs), Probate, Uncontested divorce, Landlord and Tenant disputes, Bankruptcy and so on. Within the County Court is also the Small Claims which deals with matters up to £5,000. The procedure is speedier and cheaper and the parties will be bound by the decision.

The High Court of Justice

This is divided into three divisions for administrative purposes: Queen's Bench Division, Family Division and Chancery Division.

Queen's Bench Division of the High Court

Personnel

This is the largest of the three divisions. It is headed by the Lord Chief Justice and is staffed by High Court Judges (puisne judges).

Jurisdiction

It has three types of jurisdiction.

1   *Original.* Matters involving contract and tort above the limits available in the County Court. It also has two specialist courts: Commercial and Admiralty.

2   *Appellate.* The Divisional Court of the Queen's Bench in its civil capacity hears appeals mainly from tribunals.

3   *Supervisory.* This jurisdiction is exercised by the issue of prerogative orders and the writ of habeas corpus.

The prerogative orders are as follows:

* *Mandamus* which compels a court, tribunal or public body to carry out its duty.
* *Prohibition* is used to prevent a court, tribunal or public body from exceeding its jurisdiction.
* *Certiorari* may be used to quash a decision made by a court, tribunal or public body.

Family division of the High Court Personnel

Personnel

This division is headed by a President and is staffed by High Court Judges.

Jurisdiction

The division is concerned with matrimonial disputes.

The Chancery division of the High Court

Personnel

The effective head of this division is the Vice Chancellor and it is staffed by High Court Judges.

Jurisdiction

This division deals with company and partnership law, trusts, tax, probate, mortgages and certain revenue matters. Two specialist courts – Patents and Company.

The Court of Appeal (Civil division)

Personnel

The court comprises the Master of the Rolls and Lord Justices of Appeal. A hearing is usually in the presence of three such judges.

Jurisdiction

It hears appeals from the County Court and all divisions of the High Court.

Appeals procedure

Appeal with leave is to the House of Lords (Supreme Court).

The House of Lords (The Supreme Court)

Appeals to the House of Lords are with leave of the Court below or of the House itself. On a point of law from the Court of Appeal, or directly from the High Court by the 'leapfrog' procedure.

Alternative dispute resolution

Some disputes can be resolved outside the court process and such bodies exercise important judicial functions.

Tribunals

Administrative. Set up by statute dealing with disputes arising from matters such as rent, land, social security and employment.

Domestic. Set up generally by professional bodies, for example law society, CIMA and ICAEW. All are expected to act fairly and are supervised by the Queen's Bench Division by way of prerogative orders.

Arbitration. Some commercial agreements will have a provision that in the event of a dispute between the parties it should be resolved by arbitration. Arbitration is generally quicker and cheaper than the courts. Both parties are bound by the arbitrators' decision. There is no appeal against the decision.

1

    (a)   Orders in Council are a form of ....(2 words) enacted by the .... (2 words). Individual ministers can create ministerial regulations that are also known as .... (2 words)
(3 marks)

    (b)   Parking regulations are introduced by .... (2 words) in the form of .... (1 word). Advantages of this form of law making include .... (1 word) and .... (1 word)
(4 marks)

(Total: 7 marks)

2

    (a)   Within the European Union a .... (1 word) system of law is found in a significant number of states. European Community Law became part of United Kingdom law as a result of the .... (3 words)
(2 marks)

    (b)   In the European Union the Council of Ministers makes decisions only by .... (2 words). It is the Commission that makes .... (1 word)
(6 marks)

(Total: 8 marks)

THE LAW OF CONTRACT

OFFER AND ACCEPTANCE

Offer

A contract is based on agreement. Agreement = offer + acceptance.

An offer is a definite and unequivocal statement of willingness to be bound in contract without further negotiations.

An offer must be distinguished from an invitation to treat.

Invitation to treat

This is an invitation to another party to make an offer himself. An invitation to treat cannot be 'accepted', because it is not an offer.

Examples of invitations to treat are as follows:

(a)   The display of goods in shop windows: *Fisher v Bell* 1960.

(b)   The display of goods on supermarket shelves: *Pharmaceutical Society v Boots Cash Chemists* 1953.

(c)   An answer to a request for information: *Harvey v Facey* 1893.

(d)   A declaration of intention e.g. to hold an auction: *Harrison v Nickerson* 1873.

Communication of offer to offeree

An offer can only be accepted and hence a binding contract created if it has been communicated to the offeree.

Communication may be either express (i.e. oral or written) or implied (e.g. through conduct).

An offer can be made to a specific person, to a group of people or to the world at large: *Carlill v Carbolic Smoke Ball Company* 1893.

Termination of an offer

Once terminated an offer cannot be accepted. An offer may terminate as follows:

(a)   *Lapse.* Expiry of a time limit, failure to meet a condition and death of one of the parties, or by counteroffer – change in the terms of the original offer.

(b)   *Rejection.* Rejection of the offer by the offeree. A request for further information is not an implied rejection.

(c)   *Revocation.* An offer can be withdrawn (revoked) at any time prior to acceptance, provided the offeree has not bought the offeror's promise to keep the offer open: *Routledge v Grant* 1828, but is only valid when received by the offeree.

Acceptance

Acceptance is an absolute and unqualified consent to all the terms of the offer. Any attempt to vary the terms of the offer may amount to a counteroffer, destroying the original offer. If there is no stipulated method of acceptance, then the offeree can accept by any reasonable method, which can include conduct: *Brogden v Metropolitan Railway* 1877.

If there is a stipulated method (e.g. acceptance must be in writing) then normally the offeree must use this method. Exceptions: silence cannot be an acceptance and the offeree chooses an alternative effective method of acceptance.

Effective date of acceptance

The normal rule is that acceptance is only effective when it is actually received: *Entores v Miles Far East Corporation* 1955.

An exception to this is the postal rule. Where acceptance is by post it may be effective from the moment the letter is posted even if it never reaches the offeror, provided:

(a)   the post must be stipulated or reasonable method of acceptance and

(b)   the letter must be properly addressed and properly posted.

Consideration

English law enforces bargains, not bare promises. A bare promise is unenforceable unless bought by some consideration provided by the other party. A simple definition of consideration might be 'the price of the other person's promise'.

Executory and executed consideration

Executory – means yet to be done. This means that the consideration has been promised but has yet to pass between the parties (i.e. an exchange of promises to do something in the future).

Executed – means that the consideration has passed at the time the contract is made, that is present consideration that is a promise in return for an act.

The rules on consideration

Consideration must be valuable but it need not be adequate. For example, a person who (foolishly) agrees to sell his Rolls Royce for £1 can be forced to do so, even though £1 is clearly less than adequate consideration: *Chappel v Nestle & Company* 1960 and *White v Bluett* 1853.

Consideration must be sufficient. This means that the promisor must truly incur some form of loss and that the promisee must truly gain some form of benefit. Here are some examples which do not rank as consideration:

(a)   Performance of an existing obligation imposed by law: *Collins v Godefroy* 1831 and *Glasbrook Bros v Glamorgan County Council* 1925.

(b)   Performance of an existing contractual duty owed to the other party to the contract: *Stilk v Myrick* 1809 and *Hartley v Ponsonby* 1857. However, the recent decisions in *Williams v Roffey Brothers and Nelson Contractors* 1990 appear to contradict the earlier decision in *Stilk v Myrick*.

Past consideration – 'is no consideration'

The basic rule is that consideration must pass at the time the contract is made (executed consideration) or afterwards (executory consideration), never before: *Re McArdle* 1951.

Exception – where there is an implied promise to pay: *Lampleigh v Braithwaite* 1615.

The part payment problem

The issue here is whether a creditor's promise to release his debtor from all or part of the debt can ever be legally enforceable. The rule in *Pinnel's* case 1602 states that payment of a lesser sum in satisfaction of a greater sum cannot be any consideration for the whole sum, that is it could never be sufficient consideration to support a second contract to write off the balance of the debt.

The principle was upheld in *Foakes v Beer* 1884. There are several exceptions to the rule in Pinnel's case:

(a)   Accord and satisfaction – accord means that both the parties agree freely to the part payment. Satisfaction might be payment at an earlier date, payment at a different place, payment in a different currency, payment through the giving of a chattel and so on.

(b)   Agreement by deed.

(c)   Part payment by a third party.

(d)   Composition with creditors.

(e)   Promissory estoppel.

The doctrine of promissory estoppel in equity is based on the principles of fairness and justice. The doctrine may operate to prevent a person going back on his promise to accept a lesser amount for a period of time, provided the following conditions are satisfied.

(a)   There is an existing contract between the parties;

(b)   The claimant must voluntarily waive his right under the contract;

(c)   There must be an intention that the defendant should rely on the waiver.

The principle was propounded in *Central London Property Trust v High Trees House* 1947. However, there are a number of limitations on the principle.

(a)   It is a shield not a sword, that is it is a defence not a course of action: *Combe v Combe* 1951.

(b)   It may only have a suspensory effect as shown in the High Trees Case. (The claimant's rights were suspended during the particular circumstances of the Second World War, but might be revived later.)

(c)   The party seeking to use it as an equitable defence must also have acted fairly in his dealings with the claimant: *D and C Builders v Rees* 1966.

Intention to create legal relations

For a contract to exist and be enforceable, the parties must intend to create legally binding relations between themselves. A lawful contract can exist that is not legally binding.

Commercial agreements

The legal presumption is that the parties to a commercial agreement intend to be legally bound. This can be excluded in the following ways:

(a)   By express declaration (e.g. the use of words such as 'a gentlemen's agreement', 'binding in honour only').

(b)   By the use of a *binding in honour only* clause: *Jones v Vernon Pools Ltd* 1938.

Domestic agreements

In an arrangement within a family or between friends there is a rebuttable presumption that legal relations were not intended.

Sometimes what appears to be a domestic agreement because of the relationship of the parties is actually found to be of a business nature because of the importance of money in the contract: *Simpkins v Pays* 1955.

Public duty

Where a party performs what is already a public duty this generally will not be consideration under a separate contract. For a party to receive a benefit for fulfilling the duty would amount to breach of public duty.

PRIVITY OF CONTRACT

The meaning and effect of privity

Privity of contract states that, as a general rule, a contract cannot confer rights or impose obligations on anyone except the parties to the contract. Third parties cannot sue for the carrying out of promises made by the parties to a contract.

Two cases illustrate the point: *Tweddle v Atkinson* 1861 and *Dunlop Pneumatic Tyre Company Ltd v Selfridge* 1915.

Exception to the general rule

(a)   *Trusts.* The beneficiary of a trust can enforce a trust's terms against the trustee even if the beneficiary has provided no consideration.

(b)   *Collateral Contracts.*

(c)   *Operation of law.* If the rights of one party to the contract pass by operation of law to another person, that other person may enforce those rights (e.g. when a company goes into liquidation).

(d)   *Assignment.* It is possible for one party to a contract to assign his rights and liabilities under the contract to another person, provided the other party to the contract has consented.

(e)   *Property.* The law of property has developed rules whereby a vendor of land may, as part of a contract to sell the land, impose a restriction on its use which he can enforce despite subsequent changes in ownership of the land. For example, when a house is sold it might be a condition that it can never be used for business purposes. The condition will be enforceable even against anyone who subsequently buys the house and is not a party to the contract with the original owner.

(f)   *Statutory exception.* Where a husband or wife insures his or her own life, his or her spouse and children may enforce the contract with the insurance company (Married Women's Property Act 1882).

(g)   *Contracts Rights of Third Parties Act 1999.* A third party will have a right to sue if they are given such a right in the contract or a contractual benefit. However, no such right will exist if on true construction of the contract no such right to pursue a claim was intended.

MISREPRESENTATION

Definition of a misrepresentation

In negotiations leading to a contract many statements may be made. Those statements which are incorporated into the final contract become contractual terms; those not incorporated may be representations, which if untrue are called misrepresentations. A misrepresentation is a false statement of material fact made by one party (the misrepresentor) before or at the time of the making of the contract, which was intended to (and did) induce the other party (the misrepresentee) to enter into the contract. The effect of a misrepresentation on a contract is to render it voidable (but not void), that is valid unless and until avoided.

The definition of misrepresentation can be broken down into the following elements.

A statement

Silence does not amount to a misrepresentation. Therefore in general there is no duty to volunteer information.

To this rule there are exceptions: half truths, change in circumstances, contracts of utmost good faith (contracts *uberrimae fidei*) such as insurance contracts.

A statement of fact

The statement must be of fact, not of law, opinion or intention.

The statement must be one of existing fact, not future intention. However, a statement of intention may amount to a misrepresentation if the intention was not honestly held.

A statement of fact which is false

A statement is false not only if it is untrue but where it is true but misleading in the context.

A statement made by one contracting party

The statement must be made by one of the contracting parties or his agent.

A statement which induced the other party to enter into the contract

Induced means that the statement must be one of the reasons the misrepresentee entered into the contract – it need not be the only reason.

Types of misrepresentation and remedies

(a) **Fraudulent misrepresentation** occurs where the misrepresentor knows that the statement is untrue or is reckless as to its truth or falsity. *Remedies* – the misrepresentee may either rescind the contract or claim damages for deceit.

(b) **Negligent misrepresentation** occurs where the misrepresentor believes the statement is true but does not take reasonable care to ascertain its truth or falsity. *Remedies* – the misrepresentee may claim damages either for negligence or under s2(I) Misrepresentation Act 1967.

(c) **Innocent misrepresentation** occurs where the misrepresentor is neither fraudulent nor negligent, that is he genuinely believes his statement to be true. *Remedies* – rescission or damages. However, if rescission is unavailable damages in lieu of rescission will not be granted by the court. Therefore, in some instances, there is no remedy for an innocent misrepresentation.

Rescission is an equitable remedy (and therefore discretionary) which restores the parties to their exact pre-contractual position.

There are, however, certain limitations or bars to rescission:

(a) affirmation;

(b) lapse of time;

(c) full restitution (*resitutio in integrum*) is impossible;

(d) third-party intervention.

TERMS OF A CONTRACT

Conditions and warranties

The terms of a contract define the obligations of the parties and the remedies available if either party is in breach of contract. It is usual to classify each term of a contract as being either a condition or a warranty.

Conditions are terms which are so vital to a contract that non-performance may be treated by the innocent party as a substantial failure to perform the contract (*Poussard v Spiers* 1876).

Breach of condition – the innocent party may:

(a)   Repudiate the contract and if relevant sue for damages, that is he may refuse to accept performance and treat the contract as discharged, suing for any loss he incurs as a result.

(b)   Affirm the contract and sue for damages, that is he may continue with the contract, accept performance and sue at the end for any resultant loss.

Warranties are terms which are subsidiary to the main purpose of the contract such that their non-performance does not represent a substantial failure of the contract: *Bettini v Gye* 1876.

Breach of warranty – the innocent party must affirm the contract (i.e. continue with the contract), suing at the end for any resultant loss.

Innominate terms

A third 'intermediate' type of term has been created to make the law on terms more flexible: innominate terms. These are terms whose breach may or may not cause a contract to fail substantially. This will depend on the consequences of the breach *Hong Kong Fir Shipping co ltd v Kawasaki Kisen Kaisha Ltd* 1962.

Express terms and implied terms

Express terms are terms expressly inserted into the contract by the parties. Such terms may be written, oral or a combination of both.

Implied terms are terms which have not been expressed by the parties but which for various reasons are contained within the contract. Terms may be implied into a contract by custom, by the courts or by statute.

Terms implied by custom:

Any contract may be deemed to include any relevant custom of the market.

Terms implied by the courts:

(a)   *Lack of business efficacy.* Here the court considers that the parties must have intended to include the term, because otherwise the contract would not be workable (*The Moorcock* 1889).

(b)   *By custom or trade usage.*

(c)   *Imbalance of bargaining strength.* In such a case the court may imply a term where it is just and reasonable to do so rather than strictly necessary (*Liverpool City Council v Irwin* 1977).

Terms implied by statute:

Parliament has decided that in certain types of contract the imbalance of bargaining power is so wide that statute is needed to ensure that certain terms are always implied into contracts. An example is the Sale of Goods Act 1979, which primarily seeks to protect the consumer when otherwise the rule of caveat emptor would imply (let the buyer beware).

SGA1979 implies the following conditions in contracts for the sale of goods:

- Title (Ownership);

- Description;

- Quality and Fitness Sample.

EXCLUSION CLAUSES

Validity tests

An exclusion clause is one which seeks to exclude or restrict the obligations of one of the parties under the contract.

To counter the more unfair aspects of exclusion clauses the person seeking to rely on the clause must prove that it passes various tests arising from both common law and statute.

Common law requirements

In order to be valid a first requirement is that the clause must be properly incorporated into the contract (i.e. it must be a term of the contract).

A person who signs a contractual document is bound by its terms even if he has not read them: *L'Estrange v Graucob* 1939.

A clause contained in an unsigned document will only be incorporated into the contract if 'reasonable steps' are taken before the contract is made to bring it to the attention of the party who will be prejudicially affected by it.

An exception to the above rule arises where there have been regular and consistent dealings between the parties.

If the parties have entered into a regular number of contracts over a period of time using a form with consistent terms, such terms, including an exclusion clause, might be incorporated into the agreement, even if, in an isolated case, some contractual term is missing: *Spurling v Bradshaw* 1956.

The contra proferentem rule

In order to be valid, the clause must be worded so as to exclude the loss in question.

If the wording of the clause is ambiguous the courts will interpret it contra proferentem, that is in the way least favourable to the party seeking to rely on it: *Wallis Sons & Wells v Pratt & Haynes* 1911.

Statutory requirements relating to exclusion clauses

The main source of statutory regulation in this area is the Unfair Contract Terms Act 1977 (UCTA1977).

This severely limits the ability of a party to exclude liability, both in contracts, generally and more specifically in contracts for the sale of goods.

Provisions of the 1977 Act

Clauses excluding liability in negligence are only valid in limited circumstances.

(a)   Death or personal injury – liability for negligence resulting in death or personal injury can never be excluded. Such clauses are therefore void.

(b)   Other economic loss – liability for negligence resulting in damage to property or other economic loss can be excluded but only if such exclusion is reasonable.

The following criteria under UCTA 1977 are therefore relevant in determining reasonableness.

(a)   Bargaining strength of the parties;

(b)   Choice;

(c)   Inducement;

(d)   Knowledge of the existence of the clause;

(e)   Insurance cover.

The UCTA 1977 also has relevance to the SGA 1979. Implied conditions relating to title/ownership, description, quality and fitness as well as sample can never be excluded in consumer contracts but can be excluded in a non-consumer sale but only if such exclusion is reasonable.

The Unfair Terms in Consumer Contract Regulations 1999 makes any term void if the contract was not individually negotiated and is detrimental to the consumer.

DISCHARGE OF CONTRACT

Performance

Discharge of contract releases the parties from their mutual obligations. There are various ways in which this can happen.

(a)   By performance;

(b)   By breach;

(c)   By frustration;

(d)   By agreement (i.e. the parties mutually agree to terminate their contract).

The rule on performance

The general rule is that performance must be complete, exact and precise for the contract to be discharged. Exceptions:

(a)   *Severable of divisible contracts.* For example, 100 tons of coal to be delivered in 10 ton consignments.

(b)   *Performance prevented by one party.* If one party prevents the other's performance the party not at fault can recover a reasonable sum for what he has done – *quantum meruit* (*Planche v Colburn* 1831).

(c)   *Acceptance of partial performance.* If one party freely and voluntarily accepts part performance then the other party can claim a *quantum meruit* (*Sumpter v Hedges* 1898).

(d)   *Substantial performance.* This occurs where the party has done all that was agreed but with defects (*Hoenig v Isaacs* 1952).

DISCHARGE BY EXPRESS AGREEMENT

Discharge by agreement (accord and satisfaction)

The parties may decide before either of them has performed his side of the contract that they will not perform it or that they will both do something different instead.

Their agreement to discharge the contract will be valid without any formality. The consideration is their mutual release. This is known as bilateral discharge.

Sometimes, one party will agree to excuse or release the other party from performance, even though he himself has already performed his part of the contract. This is known as unilateral discharge.

New agreement

A new agreement may be entered into by the parties to the original contract, whereby the earlier contract is replaced by a later one. This is termed 'novation'. However, this will be effective only if both parties still had to perform their obligations under the earlier contract.

Provision for discharge

A provision may be incorporated in a contract whereby the contract will automatically be discharged if:

(a)   A condition is not fulfilled, which is termed a condition precedent (*Head v Tattersall* 1871).

(b)   A certain event occurs, which is termed a condition subsequent.

(c)   The contract contains a term that either party may terminate by notice (e.g. contracts of employment).

Form of agreement to discharge

An agreement to discharge does not normally require any particular format; indeed, a contract under seal may be discharged by an oral agreement.

However, a contract which must be evidenced in writing (e.g. a money lending contract) can only be varied in writing.

FRUSTRATION

Circumstances where a contract is frustrated

This occurs where events occur after the contract has been made which make the agreement impossible to perform. These events must be brought about by external factors beyond the control of the contracting parties.

Frustration applies in the following circumstances.

(a)   Supervening illegality.

(b)   Destruction of the subject matter (*Taylor v Caldwell* 1863).

(c)   Non-occurrence of the event on which the contract is based.

(d)   Death or serious illness in a contract for personal services.

(e)   An extensive interruption which alters performance (*Metropolitan Water Board v Dick Kerr & Company* 1918).

Frustration does not apply in the following situations (i.e. these are non-frustrating events).

(a)   Self-induced frustration – this means that one party by his own choice induces impossibility which could have been avoided.

(b)   Performance becomes more difficult or expensive (*Tsakiroglou v Noblee & Thorl* 1962).

(c)   Where one party finds he cannot achieve what he has contracted to do.

The effects of frustration

Where frustration is found to exist, the provisions of the Law Reform (Frustrated Contracts) Act 1943 apply. The consequences are as follows:

(a)   All sums paid are recoverable.

(b)   All outstanding balances cease to be payable.

(c)   If one party has incurred any expenses prior to frustration, a reasonable sum may be claimed for that expenditure.

(d)   If one party has received some benefit prior to frustration, he must pay for that benefit.

Breach

Remedies for breach

Although every breach of contract entitles the innocent party to claim damages, not every breach has the effect of discharging the contract and thus releasing the innocent party from his obligations.

(a)   Breach of condition entitles the innocent party to repudiate his future obligations.

(b)   Breach of warranty only entitles the innocent party to claim damages not to repudiate.

Types of breach of condition

(a)   *Actual breach.* This is where one party refuses to perform his side of the bargain after the due date or performs incompletely. The cases of *Poussard v Spiers* and *Bettini v Gye* are examples.

(b)   *Anticipatory breach.* This is where one party announces in advance of the due date for performance, his intention not to perform his side of the bargain, either expressly or by implication. The innocent party may sue immediately for damages on the announcement of the breach.

Where the innocent party requires no further co-operation from the other party, he can elect to affirm the contract, complete his part of the agreement and claim damages: *White and Carter v McGregor* 1962.

REMEDIES FOR BREACH OF CONTRACT

Damages

This is the basic remedy available for a breach. It is a common law remedy that can be claimed as of right by the innocent party.

The object of damages is usually to put the injured party into the same financial position he would have been in if the contract had been performed properly.

Remoteness and causation

In determining the level of damages to be awarded a judge will initially consider 'remoteness of damage'. Damages will only be awarded in relation to that which arises naturally from the breach and is within the reasonable contemplation of the parties. Compensation will not be awarded where the loss identified is too remote – *Hadley v Baxendale* 1854.

A chain of causation between the breach and the damage resulting is normally anticipated. However, a break in the chain will not necessarily have an adverse effect on the claims – *Lambert v Lewis* 1981.

Measure of damages

Having determined the damage upon which compensation is to be based, a judge must then determine the actual award to be made. This is known as the measure of damages. Whilst loss of profits can be included, speculative profits cannot.

Liquidated damages and penalty clauses

The parties may agree a sum to be paid in the event of a breach. This sum may be either liquated damages or a penalty clause. Only liquidated damages are enforceable.

(a)   A liquidated damages clause is a genuine attempt at estimating the loss prior to the breach and is enforceable by either party to the contract. It does not have to be an exact figure.

(b)   Penalty clauses are clauses inserted *in terrorem*, that is to force a party to perform his obligations. The amount will be penal and thus designed to punish a party for the breach. Such clauses will not be upheld by the courts.

A clause is likely to be construed as a penalty clause if it exhibits any of the following features:

(a)   The figure stipulated is 'extravagant and unconscionable';

(b)   The figure stipulated is the same for both major and minor breaches;

(c)   Where the breach is a monetary breach, the figure stipulated is greater than the breach.

Unliquidated damages

These are damages awarded by the court in the light of the criteria outlined below. The rules for assessment of such damages were laid down in the case of *Hadley v Baxendale*. They state that the defendant will not necessarily be responsible for all the consequences of his breach as some damages may be considered too remote. The remoteness rules are as follows.

(a)   Normal loss (i.e. general damages) arises naturally from the breach such that the parties should have had it in contemplation as likely to occur as a consequence of any breach.

(b)   Abnormal loss (i.e. special damages) does not arise naturally from the breach but may still reasonably be supposed to have been in the contemplation of the parties at the time of making the contract.

The measure of damages

This is the sum required to restore the innocent party to the position he would have been in but for the breach. Therefore if there is no actual loss (e.g. because the buyer can get alternative goods more cheaply), only nominal damages are available. *Lazenby Garages v Wright* 1976.

Under the doctrine of restitution, the plaintiff is entitled to damages measured by the value to him of the contract broken, and not by the cost of performance to the defendant. The injured party should seek to minimise the loss suffered (*Brace v Calder* 1895). Although the measure of damages in contract is usually for financial loss other types of loss may also be recovered (e.g. personal injury, damage to property and mental distress such as frustration, disappointment and vexation). However, all these types of loss are subject to the rule that damages which are too remote cannot be recovered. The difficulty of accurately assessing damages is no reason for refusing to grant any compensation at all, even though the assessment of damages is almost a matter of guesswork: *Chaplin v Hicks* 1910.

Equitable remedies

As equity is based on equality, fairness and justice, then such remedies are only available where the court in its discretion considers that such a remedy is appropriate in all the circumstances of the case and is fair in relation to both parties to the agreement.

Usually the common law remedy of damages is sought for breach of contract. There are other possible remedies, however.

Specific performance

This is an equitable remedy, being an order requiring the defendant to perform the contract – only available where the goods are rare or unique.

Specific performance is not available in the following circumstances.

(a)   Damages provide an adequate remedy;

(b)   The court cannot supervise performance;

(c)   The contract is for personal services;

(d)   It would not be just and equitable;

(e)   Not mutually enforceable.

Injunction

This is an equitable remedy and like all remedies granted by equity it is discretionary and available only in equitable circumstances. It is an order restraining the defendant from breaching his contract: *Warner Bros v Nelson* 1937.

Quantum meruit

This means 'as much as he has earned' and is an equitable claim to compensate a person for a breach: *Planche v Colburn* 1831.

LIMITATION OF ACTIONS

A claim for damages which is commenced outside the statutory limitation period is barred under the Limitation Act 1980. Such a contract is unenforceable.

The time periods are as follows:

(a)   *Simple contracts* – six years.

(b)   *Specialty contracts* (i.e. contract made by deed) – twelve years.

(c)   *Personal injury or death* – three years.

The period commences on the date the contract was breached, subject to exceptions (e.g. disability or fraud).

3

(a) In Contract Law an offer can be made to the ……………….. ………………. ………………. (3 words). **(2 marks)**

(b) To be effective, an acceptance of an offer must be ………………. (1 word) and ………………. (1 word). **(2 marks)**

(c) Both parties to a contract must provide consideration, and the consideration must be………………. (1 word); however, the consideration need not be ………………. (1 word). **(2 marks)**

(Total: 6 marks)

4

(a) Promissory estoppel can only be used as a ………………. (1 word) and not a ……………….(1 word). **(2 marks)**

(b) The doctrine of promissory estoppel is based on the principles of ………………. (1 word) and its effect is only ………………. (1 word). **(2 marks)**

(Total: 4 marks)

5

(a) Where a breach of condition occurs, the innocent party can repudiate the contract and/or sue for damages. If the innocent party affirms the contract on such a breach, he can/cannot sue for damages. **(2 marks)**

(b) Contract terms can be implied at common law where there is a lack of ………………. ………………. (2 words). Terms are implied under the Sale of Goods Act 1979, which primarily seek to protect the ………………. (1 word) **(2 marks)**

(c) Without this statutory protection the rule of ………………. ………………. (2 words) which means ………………. ………………. ………………. ………………. (4 words) would apply. **(2 marks)**

(Total: 6 marks)

6

(a) Silence cannot constitute misrepresentation. However, certain exceptions to this rule exist. These include where a change ………………. ………………. (2 words) is found.

Also where a contract *uberrimae fidei* exists. This Latin term means of the ………………. ………………. ………………. (3 words). **(2 marks)**

(b) Three types of misrepresentation are recognised, innocent, negligent and ………………. (1 word). The equitable remedy of ………………. (1 word) which serves to restore the parties to the pre-contract position may be available. **(2 marks)**

(Total: 4 marks)

THE LAW OF EMPLOYMENT

EMPLOYEES AND CONTRACTORS

There are two main types of employment.

1   An employee has a contract *of* service.

2   A self-employed person has a contract *for* services.

The distinction is important for the following reasons.

(a)   Only employees are given statutory protection against unfair dismissal, redundancy and so on;

(b)   Only employees have implied into their contract certain common law duties of employer and employee;

(c)   Only employees can make their employers vicariously liable for their torts (i.e. for any damage caused by their acts or omissions);

(d)   Only employees are entitled to certain state benefits;

(e)   Employees' tax is deducted through PAYE and assessed under Schedule E;

(f)   An employer must pay National Insurance contributions in respect of every employee.

As it is not always easy to determine the difference, the courts have developed a number of tests to distinguish between workers who are employed and workers who are self-employed.

The control test

The test was set out in *Yewens v Noakes* 1880: 'a servant is a person subject to the command of his masters as to the manner in which he shall do his work.'

The integration test

This test (also called the organisation test) applies if the person's work is integrated into the business of the employer. If so, he is an employee (*Cassidy v Ministry of Health* 1951).

The economic reality test

This test looks at a number of different factors to decide on the economic reality of the working relationship. The leading case on the matter is *Ready Mixed Concrete v Minister of Social Security* 1969.

In this case it was stated that there was no exhaustive test or strict rules laid down as to factors which identified a contract of service. However, factors which will be considered include the following:

(a)   The degree of control by the employer;

(b)   The degree of risk taken by the worker;

(c)   Ownership of tools and equipment;

(d)   Regularity of payment methods;

(e)   Regularity of obligations;

(f)   Regularity of hours;

(g)   Ability to provide a substitute.

Formation of the employment contract

The contract will consist of express terms, implied terms and statutory terms.

(a)   *Express terms.* Under the Employment Rights Act 1996 a statement of particulars must be given by the employer to the employee within two months of the commencement of employment. This must cover details such as pay, holidays, job title and so on.

(b)   *Implied terms.* Certain terms are implied into the employment contract by the common law and the courts, even if they are not expressly stated.

(c)   *Statutory terms.* Terms relating to employment are laid down in the Equal Pay Act 1970, the Sex Discrimination Act 1975 and other legislation.

DUTIES OF EMPLOYERS AND EMPLOYEES

Duties of the employers

(a)   A duty to pay reasonable remuneration;

(b)   A duty to indemnify the employee for reasonably incurred expenses in the performance of his duties;

(c)   A duty to provide a safe system of work;

(d)   A duty to give reasonable notice of termination of employment;

(e)   A duty of mutual co-operation, trust, confidence and respect.

Duties of the employees

(a)   A duty to obey lawful reasonable orders;

(b)   A duty of mutual co-operation, that is to perform work in a reasonable manner;

(c)   A duty to exercise reasonable care and skill;

(d)   A duty of good faith, that is a duty to give loyal and faithful service. This duty includes the following:

   1   Not to make a secret profit: *Boston Deep Sea Fishing and Ice Company v Ansell* 1888.

   2   Not to compete with his employer's business: *Hivac Limited v Park Royal Scientific Instruments Limited* 1946.

   3   Not to disclose trade secrets or misuse confidential information.

(e)   A duty to render personal service, that is not to delegate the performance of his work.

TERMINATION OF EMPLOYMENT

Methods of terminating the contract

(a)   *Termination without notice by the employer.* This is called summary dismissal and may be justified if the conduct of the employee prevents the continuance of employment.

(b)   *Termination without notice by the employee.* This is often a breach of contract unless the behaviour of the employer justifies the act (e.g. constructive dismissal).

(c)   *Termination with notice.* A notice period may be agreed expressly or by implication but cannot be less than the statutory minimum. When a fixed-term contract expires no notice is required.

(d)   *Termination by agreement.*

(e)   *Termination by operation of law.* For example, through frustration or dissolution.

Breach of contract

In some cases, termination of employment will constitute a breach of contract.

(a)   The employee will be in breach of contract if he terminates his employment without giving the agreed notice or breaches some other term of his contract. The employer may then dismiss the employee without notice if the breach is serious and can sue for damages.

(b)   The employer may be in breach in cases of summary dismissal or constructive dismissal.

Constructive dismissal refers to situations where an employer makes it practically impossible for an employee to continue in his job, without actually dismissing him (*Donovan v Invicta Airways* 1970).

The employee's remedies are as follows:

(a)   If he was dismissed correctly, with proper notice, he has no claim against the employer.

(b)   If he was dismissed rightfully, but without proper notice, he may sue for unpaid wages.

(c)   If he was dismissed wrongfully, and without proper notice, he can claim wages due plus damages for wrongful dismissal, or a *quantum meruit* payment, or an injunction against the employer.

Note that damages are compensatory and may be reduced if the employee fails to mitigate his loss: *Brace v Calder* 1895.

Unfair dismissal

Here the employer terminates the contract without justifiable reason. Only employees who qualify can claim, therefore the following criteria must be established.

(a)   The employee must not be over retirement age;

(b)   He must have been continuously employed for at least one year;

(c)   He must have made a claim to the Industrial Tribunal within three months;

(d)   He must prove he was dismissed.

The employer, to defend himself, must show that the main reason for dismissal was one which is permitted under statute.

The five permitted reasons are as follows:

1   Lack of capabilities or qualifications to perform the kind of work he is required to do;

2   Misconduct;

3   Redundancy;

4   Where continued employment would contravene a statute;

5   Some other substantial reason – of a kind such as to justify the dismissal of an employee.

Reasonableness

Once the employee has shown he was dismissed and the employer has shown it was for one of the five reasons outlined above it is then for the tribunal to decide whether the dismissal was fair on reasonableness grounds.

Inadmissible reasons

The Employment Rights Act 1996 sets out a number of reasons on which the employer is not allowed to rely to justify the dismissal. This is very important because the following consequences ensue if the employer seeks to rely on one of the inadmissible reasons.

(a)   The dismissal is automatically unfair, and the reasonableness test is not relevant;

(b)   The qualifying conditions of age and continuous service do not have to be satisfied;

(c)   The monetary awards are higher than for other reasons.

The following are inadmissible reasons for dismissal.

(a)   Complaints by an employee on health and safety matter;

(b)   Pregnancy or childbirth;

(c)   Trade unionism or refusal to join a trade union, or take part in its activities;

(d)   Assertion of a statutory right (rights given under Employment Rights Act 1996);

(e)   Unfair selection for redundancy (e.g. selection in contravention of agreed procedures or if the reason for selection was inadmissible).

If the dismissal was unfair the tribunal may order a re-instatement, re-engagement or compensation.

(a)   Re-instatement means that the employee is given his job back.

(b)   Re-engagement means that the employee is given a different job under a new contract.

(c)   If either of the above is not awarded then the tribunal may order compensation to be paid. This is made up of three awards: the basic award, the compensatory award and the additional award.

   1   *Basic award.* This depends on the age of the employee, his weekly pay and the length of his continuous service. See notes on redundancy.

   2   *Compensatory award.* This is a discretionary award and is based on the employee's losses and expenses (e.g. wages, pension rights, etc.).

   3   *Additional award.* This is a special award of a higher amount, and is given:

   •   where the employee ignores an order for re-instatement or re-engagement

   •   where the dismissal is unfair because of unlawful race or sex discrimination

   •   where the reason cited for dismissal is an inadmissible one.

DISCRIMINATION IN EMPLOYMENT

Sex Discrimination Acts, 1975 and 1986

Sex Discrimination (Amendment of Legislation) Regulations 2008

Prohibits discrimination on the grounds of sex or marital status at all stages of employment including:

(a) advertising a post;

(b) selection of post;

(c) promotion and training;

(d) dismissal.

The Acts apply equally to discrimination against men and women. Discrimination may be both direct and indirect.

Direct – a woman on the grounds of her sex is treated less favourably than a man. The motive behind the discrimination is irrelevant.

Indirect – where an employer imposes a condition or requirement for a job that a large proportion of women would be unable to comply with: *Price v Civil Service* 1978.

It is not unlawful to discriminate where a person's sex is a genuine qualification for the job.

(a) Characteristics – model;

(b) Authenticity – actor;

(c) Decency or Privacy.

Action: in a tribunal for discrimination or unfair dismissal.

Race Relations Act, 1976

Prohibits discrimination whether direct or indirect on the grounds of colour, race, nationality or ethnic or national origins at all stages of employment.

It is not unlawful to discriminate where a person's race is a genuine occupational qualification. This will be for reasons of authenticity in artist's or photographer's models.

Action: in a tribunal for discrimination or unfair dismissal.

Disability Discrimination Act, 1995

Prohibits direct discrimination on the grounds of disability at all stages of employment. The act applies where an employer employs 15 or more people.

It is not unlawful to discriminate where the employer believes that the nature of the disability substantially affects the disabled persons' ability to perform the job.

Equal Pay Act, 1970 as amended

Prohibits pay differentials between male and female employees at the same workplace, that is if they do 'like work', work rated as equivalent and work of equal value: *Hayward v Cammell Laird* 1988. An employer may justify differentials if he can show a 'genuine material difference', for example experience, productivity or qualifications.

Employment Equality (Age) Regulations 2006 and Amendment Regulations 2008

The Regulations made it unlawful to discriminate against any employee on the basis of age. Direct or indirect discrimination on the basis of age are prohibited. Certain exceptions are identified under these Regulations.

OCCUPATIONAL SAFETY

Legislative controls

Common Law controls were found principally in the tort of negligence. Significant statutory development was established with the introduction of the Health and Safety at Work Act 1974. Subsequent related Regulations also made an impact. Under this Act, a general duty is attached to employers and also those who are in control of premises, manufacturers, suppliers, the self-employed and employees.

In more recent times, further change has been introduced following directives aimed at achieving uniformity in health and safety requirements across the European Union. Ongoing changes were introduced through Regulations and codes of practice made in the 1990s and culminating in 1996. Much legislation established prior to the Health and Safety at Work Act 1974, which includes the Factories Act 1961 and the Offices, Shops and Railway Premises Act 1963 have been replaced.

Six directives led to the introduction of six separate Regulations. One of the six was the Management of Health and Safety at Work Regulations 1992 under which employers have a clear duty to carry out a risk assessment related to health and safety. Beyond this, employers must reduce or remove these risks. Along with the five further Regulations introduced, the collective effect has been to replace the patchwork collection of legislation applicable in this area.

Enforcement of the Health and Safety at Work Act 1974 and related legislation attaches to the Health and Safety Commission which acts through the Health and Safety Executive and its inspectorate. The inspectors have the right of power and investigation. They can also issue improvement notices and prohibition notices. Criminal proceedings can also be instigated where appropriate.

Under the Health and Safety (Offences) Act 2008 existing maximum penalties for certain health and safety offences were extended.

Civil liability for occupational injuries

Employer liability can arise as a result of his own acts or the acts of employees where vicarious liability attaches. A liability to provide statutory sick pay will arise along with possibly a compensation payment. Claims can be commenced in contract law, the tort of negligence or breach of statutory duty. An employer owes a duty of care to employees. This duty requires the employer to act 'so far as is reasonably practicable'. This can be seen as aligning with the common law demand of displaying reasonable care. The employer has duties specifically related to firstly, selection of staff, secondly provision of materials, machinery and equipment and thirdly, to establish a safe system of working involving staff and equipment.

Contributory negligence can be pleaded by employers in both negligence and breach of statutory duty claims. In consequence, damages payable can be reduced.

7

    (a)   When considering the question of whether or not a worker is an employee or an independent contractor, the economic reality test can be used in arriving at a decision.   Factors relevant when applying this test include regularity of ……………….. ………………., (2 words) and ……………… (1 word) and ……………… (1 word). A further test that is relevant is known as the Integration test. This is sometimes also referred to as the ……………….. ……………….. (2 words)   **(4 marks)**

    (b)   Whilst an employee has a contract (2 words), an independent contractor has a contract ……………….. ……………….. (2 words)   **(2 marks)**

                                                                          (Total: 6 marks)

8

    (a)   Employers can be ……………… (1 word) liable for the ……………… (1 word) of employees.   **(2 marks)**

    (b)   The Equal Pay Act 1970 prohibits pay differentials between male and female employees. An exception exists, however, where the employer can show a ……………….. ……………….. ……………… (3 words).   **(2 marks)**

                                                                          (Total: 4 marks)

COMPANY ADMINISTRATION

THE COMPANIES ACT 2006

The Companies Act 2006 contains 1,300 sections and 16 Schedules. It is a consolidating Act and replaces the Companies Act 1985. Since becoming law, the Act has been implemented in a piecemeal manner.

Changes under the CA2006 will have an effect on:

- Company formation and documentation;
- Company names;
- The memorandum of association;
- The articles of association;
- Share capital;
- Maintenance of capital;
- Company provision of financial assistance;
- Meetings and resolutions;
- Form of communication with members;
- Director duties;
- Minority shareholder protection and derivative actions;
- The company secretary; and
- Company records and accounts.

THE NATURE OF A COMPANY AND INCORPORATION

The consequences of incorporation

Types of business organisation. The principle legal forms of business organisation used in Great Britain are:

(a)   Sole trader

(b)   Partnership

(c)   Corporation.

Sole traders

A sole trader is so called because he alone bears the responsibility for running the business and he alone takes the profit.

Sole traders can use a 'business name'. To do this, rules in s's 1192 -1208 CA2006 must be complied with. The name of the business owner must be stated on all business documentation. This is because the business name is not the name of an entity recognised at law. In any proceedings it will be the owner who would be liable in the event of e.g. a breach of contract or negligence. Restrictions on the use of particular names exist. This is particularly evident where the name selected does not reveal the nature of the actual entity. The word company can be used in the business name of a sole trader.

Partnership

Partnership is defined by s1 of the Partnership Act 1890 as 'the relation which subsists between persons carrying on a business in common with a view of profit'.

Partnership law, that is the law governing such associations and now largely codified by the Partnership Act 1890, is based on the law of agency, each partner being at one and the same time both the principal and the agent of the other(s).

A partnership does not have a separate legal personality. Partnerships are not legal entities distinct and separate from the persons of which they consist, their business and personal affairs are not separate. Partnership property will belong to the partners jointly.

A partnership does not require any formality to set up, in the sense there is no legal obligation for a Partnership document. Consequently, a partnership can be formed orally, by conduct or in writing. Not being a separate legal entity, the liability of the partners is unlimited and is joint and several. Partners are jointly and severally liable for claims in tort and contract. Even a person who is not a partner can be liable e.g. a retired partner who has not given sufficient notice of retirement or someone who wrongly represented themselves as a partner.

A partnership can use a 'firm name'. In selecting a name, caution must be had in avoiding the possibility being liable in the tort of 'passing-off'. This will occur if the name is similar to the name of a competitor.

Professional regulations may exist and apply to the partnership e.g. a firm of accountants. Beyond this, however, very limited external regulation applies to the partnership.

Generally a partnership can be dissolved very easily. One partner can give notice of their intention to leave the partnership. This in turn would bring the partnership to an end. The death or bankruptcy of a partner will automatically bring about termination of the partnership.

A partner is an agent of the firm. The firm will therefore be liable to an outsider with a valid claim where the relevant partner acts within their apparent authority.

Limited Liability Partnership. The Limited Liability Partnership (LLP) Act 2000 came into force on 1 April 2001 and allows for the creation of a new form of business entity.

An Incorporation document must be filed at the Companies House stating

(a)   The name of the firm which must end in LLP;

(b)   Location of the registered office i.e. England, Scotland or Wales;

(c)   Address of the registered office;

(d)   Name of the members (Partners) on Incorporation.

A Limited Liability Partnership is a separate legal entity distinct from its members. The firms' liability is unlimited. The members have limited liability. It is a cross between a Company and a Partnership.

Debts will normally be LLP debts. It can pursue any commercial objects and there is no limit to the number of its members. Whilst its members will have limited liability, the LLP will have to submit an annual return and audited accounts to the Registrar of Companies.

The LLP is not subject to statutory obligations for meetings or types of resolutions. Also it does not have a board of directors. Many LLP's are formed by professional practices wanting the protection of limited liability.

The registered company. A registered company is a form of corporate body and as such has a legal identity distinct from the persons of which it is composed. It acquires its corporate status by registration under the Companies Act 2006.

Corporation

A corporation is an artificial legal person. A legal person is any entity, human or otherwise, which is accepted by the law as having certain defined rights and duties; it is capable of being the subject and object of legal rights and duties.

Incorporation, the process conferring corporate status, results in the corporation being recognised by the law as having a legal personality separate and distinct from its human members. This factor was first fully recognised as regards registered companies in the famous case of *Salomon v Salomon and Co Limited* 1897.

There are two kinds of corporation – the corporation sole and the corporation aggregate.

1   A corporation sole is a perpetual office, such as the Crown, having one human member at any one time: the association is successive.

2   A corporation aggregate is composed of a number of persons associated together. Registered companies are one kind of corporation aggregate.

Although incorporation under the Companies Act is the most common form of incorporation, it is not the only way in which a company may be formed. Corporate status may be acquired in any of the following ways.

(a)   *By royal charter.* Bodies acquiring corporate status in this way are technically termed 'chartered corporation'. Examples include the BBC, the Association of Chartered Certified Accountants and the Institute of Chartered Accountants in England and Wales.

(b)   *By statute.*

   1   By a private (or local) Act – this method is used for the incorporation of public utility companies.

   2   By a (special) public Act – nationalised industries formed in this way are known as public corporations.

(c)   *By registration in compliance with statutory requirements.*

Companies formed in this way under CA2006 or one of the earlier Acts are called 'registered companies'.

The veil of incorporation

A company is a legal person in its own right distinct from its members. This fundamental principle can be illustrated by the following cases.

(a)   *Salomon v Salomon & Company Limited* 1897.

(b)   *Macaura v Northern Assurance* 1925.

However the concept of a veil of incorporation is a legal fiction, and so in certain circumstances the veil has been lifted by Parliament and the courts. In other words, there are sometimes grounds for treating a company and its owners as being the same, usually to prevent the owners from making unfair use of a legal technicality.

S213 Insolvency Act 1986 – fraudulent trading

Where the company is in the course of being wound up, if it appears to the court that the company business has been carried on with the intent to defraud creditors, the court may order the persons responsible (i.e. normally the owners) to make contributions to the company's debt.

S214 Insolvency Act 1986 – wrongful trading

Where a company has gone into insolvent liquidation and is in the course of being wound up and it appears to the court that the company's business has been carried on wrongfully, the court can order the directors to make contributions to the company's debt incurred after wrongful trading commenced.

S1295, Sch 16 CA2006 – wrongful use of the company name

If an officer signs a document where the company's name is incorrectly stated, he is personally liable if the company defaults.

In the above situations, the grounds for lifting the veil of incorporation come from statute. There are also situations where case law has the same effect.

(a)   Where the company is a sham (*Gilford Motor Company v Horne* 1933).

(b)   Where it is in the public interest (*Daimler Company Limited v Continental Tyre & Rubber Company Limited* 1916).

(c)   Where the company is a quasi-partnership (*Ebrahimi v Westbourne Galleries* 1973).

S761 CA2006 – public company without a trading certificate

Where a public company trades without having a trading certificate the directors can be personally liable for the corporate debt arising.

Further examples are found in:

- Fraud or sham cases;

- European Union law cases involving competition controls;

- Times of war or other emergency, and

- Inland revenue cases.

Advantages of separate legal personality

(a) Limited liability – each member of a limited company is liable to contribute only the amount he has agreed to pay on his shares.

(b) Perpetual succession.

(c) Transferability of interest.

(d) Company owns its own assets – the assets and liabilities attach to the company as a separate entity, not to its owners.

(e) Company may sue and be sued.

(f) Ease of borrowing (the floating charge).

(g) No maximum number of members.

Disadvantages of separate legal personality

(a) Formality – documents required.

(b) Publicity – accounts, business details.

(c) Expenses – Registrar's fees, auditors and so on.

(d) Subject to technical rules – capital maintenance.

Types of registered company

(a) *Public limited company.* Limited by shares only.

(b) *Private limited company.* Limited by shares or guarantee.

    1 By shares – The liability of members to contribute to the debts of the company is limited to any amount unpaid on their shares.

    2 By guarantee – The members undertake to pay a stipulated amount in the event of the company's liquidation.

(c) *Private unlimited company.* Unlimited companies are liable for their own debts but on a winding up the members are liable to contribute without limit to the assets of the company for settlement of creditors.

(d) *Single-member companies.* A company with one member who can also be the sole director is now permitted. The creation of such a company has been possible since the introduction of the Companies (Single Member Private Limited Company) Regulations 1992. This single member/director company raises issues in relation to the statutory need for meetings. A sole director may hold a meeting, equally for a shareholder meeting, one member present satisfies the quorum. A written resolution can be passed by a sole member.

(e) *Holding and subsidiary companies.* A holding company has control over a subsidiary company. This control is identified, either through the holding of more than 50% of the subsidiary company equity share capital, or having control of the board of the subsidiary company.

(f)   *Quoted companies.* Have securities quoted on a listed stock exchange.

(g)   *Community interest companies.* Company activities are aimed at being of benefit to the community. Surplus profits should be reinvested. Since 2004 it has been possible to make an application to the Regulator for community interest company status.

(h)   *European companies.* A European company is formed under European law. It must be a public company and operate in at least two states of the European Union. It has been possible to form this type of company since 2004.

(i)   *Small companies.* Compliance with certain statutory obligations can be avoided by small companies, e.g. no need to file a directors' report and need only to file a shortened balance sheet. The requirements for this type of company are satisfied if two of the following three factors are satisfied -

1   No more than 50 employees.

2   Balance sheet assets of no more than £1.4 million.

3   Turnover not in excess of £2.8 million.

COMPARISON OF PUBLIC AND PRIVATE COMPANIES

Public	*Private*
Must be limited	May be limited
Must be limited by shares (see below)	May be limited by shares or guarantee (see below)
Able to offer its shares and debentures for sale to the public	Cannot offer its shares and debentures for sale to the public
Must have an issued share capital with a nominal value of at least £50,000	No minimum issued share capital
Memorandum must state it is a public company	Memorandum does not state it is private
Name must end with the words 'public limited company'	Name must end with the word 'limited', unless it is an unlimited company
Minimum of two directors	Can have a sole director
Must have a qualified company secretary	No requirement to have a company secretary, but can decide to appoint to this position
	A sole director cannot also be company secretary
Minimum of two members, no upper limit	Minimum of one member, no upper limit

COMPARISON BETWEEN COMPANIES AND PARTNERSHIPS

Company	*Partnership*
Created by registration with a written constitution	No special formality required
Separate legal person. Company owns its property, can sue and be sued in contract	Not a separate legal person, partners own property, and are liable on contracts
Shares transferable	Limits on the transfer of shares Partnership may have to be dissolved
No maximum number of members	Normal maximum is 20
Can create fixed and floating charges	Fixed charges only
Management by directors	Management by partners
Company liable for debts	Partners personally liable for debts
Disclosure rules	Private affair
Formal dissolution procedure	May dissolve by agreement

FORMATION AND PROMOTION OF COMPANIES

Anyone intending to form and register a new company must file the following documents with the Registrar of Companies:

(a)   A memorandum of association and application for registration;

(b)   Articles of association: this is the company constitution;

(c)   Signed statement of first director(s) and secretary(ies): this includes their name, address, nationality, age, occupation and the address of the registered office;

(d)   Statutory declaration by either a solicitor, a director or the secretary that registration requirements of the Companies Acts have been complied with;

(e)   The registration fee.

Public companies have to obtain a s761 CA2006 trading certificate. For this to be obtained the directors must file a statutory declaration with the Registrar stating:

(a)   that the nominal value of allotted share capital is not less than £50,000;

(b)   that at least 25 per cent of the nominal value of each share has been paid up plus all of any premium on each share;

(c)   the amount of preliminary expenses (i.e. the costs of forming the company);

(d)   the amount of benefit given to promoters.

If a public limited company commences trading without first obtaining a s761 certificate, the consequences are as follows:

(a)   It is a criminal offence by the company and its officers;

(b)   Contracts with third parties are still binding on the company;

(c)   Directors are personally liable if the company fails to perform the contract;

(d)   If a certificate is not obtained for 12 months or more it is a ground for compulsory liquidation.

RE-REGISTRATION OF COMPANIES

A private company may re-register as a public company by following certain procedures.

(a)   Type of resolution – special resolution with consent of 75 per cent of members attending the meeting.

(b)   Required to alter – memorandum and articles of association.

(c)   Documents to be filed with the Registrar – application form, new memorandum and articles of association, copy of latest balance sheet dated not more than 7 months before the application, auditors' report, statement of auditors, declaration of compliance from directors.

(d)   Special requirements – the company must have a minimum issued share capital of £50,000 of which 25 per cent has been paid up plus the whole of any premium.

A public company may re-register as private. The procedures are as follows:

(a)   Resolution required – special resolution.

(b)   Required to alter – memorandum and articles of association.

(c)   Documents to be filed with the Registrar – application form, printed copy of the new memorandum and articles of association.

(d)   Right of objection – court proceedings can be brought by at least 50 members or holders of 5 per cent or more of the issued shares within 28 days of the special resolution.

PROMOTERS

There is no statutory definition of a promoter. However, in simple terms a promoter is a person who decides to form a company and takes the steps to set it going.

Duties of a promoter

A promoter stands in a fiduciary relationship with the company he is promoting. This means that

*   He is in a position of trust and must act in good faith in the best interests of the company.
*   He has a general duty of care and skill.
*   He has a fiduciary duty not to make a secret profit.

Any profit made must be disclosed to and approved by:

(a)   an independent board of directors and/or

(b)   the members and

(c)   potential members via a prospectus.

Possible liabilities of promoters

Pre-incorporation contracts. A company cannot contract prior to incorporation as it does not exist and therefore has no contractual capacity. The contract is therefore between the promoter and the third party: *Kelner v Baxter* 1866. The availability of Companies House satellite offices, technology and same day incorporation reduces greatly the potential for liability under pre-incorporation contracts arising.

Solutions for the promoter

(a)   Adoption of contracts by the company after incorporation, leaving contracts as non-binding options in the meantime.

(b)   Assignment of contracts by promoters to the company after incorporation.

(c)   An agreement of novation – after incorporation the company makes a new contract on the same terms as the old with the agreement of the other party.

(d)   Setting up an off-the-shelf (i.e. ready-made) company.

Advantages of a ready-made company

(a)   Cheap and simple.

(b)   Can trade immediately.

(c)   No pre-incorporation contracts.

Disadvantages of a ready-made company

Needs to deal with administrative matters.

MEMORANDUM AND ARTICLES OF ASSOCIATION

The memorandum of association

Under the CA2006 the memorandum of association is no longer the prominent document of a company and is no longer the principal element of a company's constitution. The articles of association become the dominant document. A memorandum is still required, but with the process of registration required, it is a record of the initial subscribers and their request that the company be incorporated. The memorandum is in a prescribed form. It must be delivered to the Registrar with an application for registration of the company. The application must identify the company name, situation of registered office, if the company is to be limited by shares or guarantee and if it is to be a public or private company. Further, a statement of capital must be provided if the company is to have a share capital.

The name clause

Statute imposes restrictions on the choice of name for a company. If it is a private company then its name must end with the word 'Limited' or its abbreviation 'Ltd'. The name of a public company must end with the words 'public limited company' or the abbreviation 'plc'.

A company shall not be registered with a name:

(a)   that is the same as the one appearing on the index maintained by the Registrar of Companies

(b)   if the use of the name would be a criminal offence or is offensive (e.g. words associated with charities or formed for illegal purposes)

(c)   which would be likely to give the impression that the company is in any way connected with the government

(d)   closely resembling that of an established business.

Certain words are conditionally prohibited and can only be used on obtaining the appropriate permission.

Change of name

- *Voluntary* – this requires the passing of a special resolution and application to the Registrar.
- *Mandatory* – this may be ordered by the Secretary of State if the name is the same or similar to an existing or registered name, or if it is misleading and therefore liable to cause harm to the public. It may also arise from a successful passing off action.

Business Names

A business can trade under a name other than its own (e.g. A Smith Limited can trade as Sunshine Tours). Legislation requires any company trading under a business name to disclose the true corporate name (A Smith Limited) on all business documents and at every place of business. In relation to business name usage, the same prohibitions relating to company name apply.

The objects clause

This clause sets out the limits of the company's permissible activities. Acts outside these purposes are known as *ultra vires*, that is beyond the powers of the company. Although a transaction may be *ultra vires*, the transaction is valid as regards third parties enabling an outsider to enforce it against the company. Under the CA2006, an objects clause of an existing company becomes a provision of the articles (s28 CA2006). The *ultra vires* doctrine is now of limited significance in relation to companies because they have unrestricted powers at law unless the articles contain specific restrictions (s31 CA2006). Objects content can be deleted by passing a special resolution. However, the CA2006 provides for article content that is entrenched, in which case removal can only be achieved if relevant conditions and/or procedural requirements are met.

Ultra vires remains of significance in relation to the conduct of directors.

The contractual effect of the memorandum and articles

The articles comprise the internal regulations of the company and deal with such matters as the rights of shareholders, procedure at meetings, appointment and removal of directors. Articles bind the company and the members to the same extent as if they had been signed and sealed by each member, that is they take effect as a contract. Articles can constitute a contract between each individual member and every other member: *Rayfield v Hands* 1960. Articles cannot constitute a contract between a company and any member pursuing a claim based in a capacity other than that of member: *Eley v Positive Life Assurance Co* 1876. Under previous legislation, the memorandum was identified as being a contract in relation to certain parties. This status of the document will not prevail under the CA2006. The articles become the dominant document and retain the role of a contract as well as containing the company constitution. The statutory contract between the members and the company is now identified in s33 CA2006. The memorandum, whilst necessary along with an application for registration on company formation, will merely serve as an 'historic document'.

Alteration of the articles

By s21 CA2006 a company has a general power to alter its articles by passing a special resolution. There is no statutory provision for a dissenting minority to appeal against a change.

Restrictions on altering the articles

The general power as outlined above is subject to numerous overriding restrictions.

(a) The alteration must not conflict with Companies Acts or other relevant laws.

(b) The number of shares which a member is bound to subscribe for may not be increased without his consent.

(c)   The alteration must be *bona fide* for the benefit of the company as a whole.

(d)   No alteration is permitted that increases shareholder financial liability to the company.

(e)   On any alteration a minority action could be brought under C.A. 2006 Sec. 994 on the basis of unfairly prejudicial treatment.

The alteration must not amount to a fraud on the minority.

An alteration which causes a breach of contract with an outsider is valid, but the company will be liable to pay damages: *Southern Foundries v Shirlaw* 1940.

MEETINGS AND RESOLUTIONS

Meetings

General meetings are meetings of the whole company of which there are two types.

1   An Annual General Meeting

2   General Meeting.

In addition, there are class meetings and board meetings.

S336 CA2006 requires all public companies to hold an Annual General Meeting within 6 months of the end of its accounting reference date.

Notice of the meeting and resolutions to be moved must be given to the members.

Members who alone or together hold a minimum 5% of the total voting rights, alternatively at least 100 members who have paid on average £100 and have the right to vote, may propose a resolution.

Following the introduction of the CA2006, the need for private companies to hold Annual General Meetings is removed. Prior to implementation of this Act, private companies could only dispense with this requirement if all members agreed.

Directors must give at least 21 clear days notice of the meeting.

General Meetings

Held whenever business arises between AGMs which requires members' approval.

The agenda being the reason for calling the meeting.

The notice period is 14 days. Shorter notice has to be agreed by a majority of members who hold at least 90% of the total voting power. A minimum 95% is required in the case of a plc.

The board can call such a meeting, or members holding 10 per cent of the voting share capital, or the court can order one.

Class meetings

Held whenever business arises which affects a particular class of shareholders.

The agenda usually being the variation of class rights.

The notice period is 14 days unless 95 per cent of the voting shareholders agree to a shorter notice.

The board can call such a meeting, or members holding 10% of the voting share capital can request the meeting, or the court can order one.

Board meetings

These are called by directors. Reasonable notice should be given.

Decisions are by majority.

Such meetings are called to make collective decision on important decisions concerning the running of the company.

The board may elect a Managing Director who has the authority over the day-to-day running of the company.

Resolutions

Both public and private companies can pass the following resolutions.

Special Resolutions

Requires a 75 per cent majority of members who are entitled to and do vote or by proxy. Same notice as for a meeting, that is AGM 21 days, GM 14 days.

Must be filed with the Registrar within 15 days of being passed.

Used for changing the company name, altering the articles, reducing share capital and winding up the company.

Ordinary resolutions

Require a simple majority on a show of hands or proxy. Same notice as for a meeting, that is AGM 21 days, GM 14 days.

No general requirement to file but must for increasing share capital and granting authority for directors to allot shares – Filing within 15 days.

Used for declaring a dividend, appointment of directors and auditors' approval of the accounts and any other business not specifically requiring a special resolution.

Some ordinary resolutions require special notice of 28 days from the proposer to the Company, and are used for removal, and in some instances appointment of directors and auditors.

Written resolutions

(a)   Do not require a meeting and can be used by private companies.

(b)   A written ordinary resolution requires a majority vote. A written special resolution can be passed with a minimum 75% support.

(c)   A written resolution is passed when the required majority have signified approval.

(d)   Can be used for all types of resolutions except ordinary resolutions with special notice.

Communication with members

Companies are permitted to communicate electronically with members, subject to articles content or shareholder approval at company meeting. Any such information provided must also be provided on request, free of charge to any member or debenture holder.

9

   (a)   There are two kinds of corporation, the corporation .... (1 word) and the corporation .... (1 word). **(2 marks)**

   (b)   The registered company is one kind of corporation................... (1 word). The registered company is an artificial ....(2 words). **(2 marks)**

   (c)   A veil of incorporation is recognised when a company is registered. However, this veil will be lifted under Sec. 213 Insolvency Act 1986 due to any .... (1 word) trading being found and Sec. 214 Insolvency Act 1986 where .... (1 word) trading is found. **(2 marks)**

(Total: 6 marks)

10

   (a)   Under the Companies Act 2006 it is the .... (3 words) that sets out the company's constitution. Public and private companies must have a certificate of incorporation. In addition, a public company must have a .... (2 words) before it can commence commercial activity. **(2 marks)**

   (b)   A private company can be re-registered as a public company on the passing of a/an .... (1 word) resolution. Equally, a public company can be re-registered as a private company. An objection can be brought by a minimum 50 members or the holders of at least 5%/10%/15%/20% issued shares . **(2 marks)**

(Total: 4 marks)

COMPANY FINANCE AND MANAGEMENT

SHARE CAPITAL

A company may issue to its members or the public either share capital or loan capital (debentures), or both.

The terminology of share capital

(a)   Authorised share capital means the total amount of share capital which the company is authorised to issue.

(b)   Issued share capital is the nominal value of shares which have been issued to members.

(c)   Called-up share capital is the aggregate amount which a member is required to pay for his shares. Full payment may not always be due at the time that the shares are issued.

(d)   Paid-up share capital is the aggregate amount of money paid up on shares.

(e)   Reserve capital is capital which the company has resolved not to call except in the course of winding up (i.e. uncalled capital).

ALLOTMENT OF SHARES

Procedures before allotment

The authorised share capital can be increased by ordinary resolution: s121 CA85. A copy of the memorandum plus the ordinary resolution must be sent to the Registrar within 15 days.

Directors' authority to allot shares (s's 550 and 551 CA2006)

The director of a company may not generally allot shares unless they are authorised to do so by the articles or by ordinary resolution. The directors' authority may be general or specific to a particular issue.

(a)   It must state the maximum number of shares which may be allotted and the date on which the authority expires.

(b)   It must not generally be for a period of more than five years.

(c)   It may be revoked at any time or varied by the members in a general meeting by ordinary resolution.

Directors' duties

The purpose of issuing shares is to raise capital and an issue for any other reason can be challenged.

Shares issued for the following reasons are, therefore, for improper purposes.

(a)   To facilitate a takeover: *Howard Smith v Ampol Petroleum* 1974.

(b)   To defeat a takeover: *Hogg v Cramphorn* 1967. However, consent of the members can be obtained at a general meeting: *Bamford v Bamford* 1970.

(c)   To dilute a member's voting power: *Clemens v Clemens* 1976.

Pre-emption rights (s561 CA2006)

Where a company, public or private, issues equity shares wholly for cash it must first offer them to existing equity shareholders in proportion to the nominal value of their equity holding. The holders of registered shares must receive notice in writing, and they have 21 days to take up or reject the offer.

Disapplication of pre-emption rights (s's 564, 565 and 565 CA2006)

Directors need not first offer shares to existing members in the following circumstances.

(a)   If the shares are subscriber shares, or for an employee share scheme, or bonus shares.

(b)   If the shares are issued for non-cash consideration.

Procedures on allotment

The law regards the issued share capital of a company as a buffer for the creditors. Consequently, many of the rules relating to consideration for shares are designed to ensure that shares are not issued for an inadequate capital contribution.

If a company issues shares for a consideration in excess of their nominal value, s130 CA85 requires the premium to be credited to a share premium account. This is a capital account and is not distributable to members. It is treated as part of the paid up capital and may not be depleted. However, the share premium account can be used for certain purposes defined in statute.

(a)   To write-off expenses on the incorporation of the company (known as preliminary expenses).

(b)   To write-off the discount on the issue of debentures.

(c)   To write-off underwriting commission.

(d)   To write-off a premium on the redemption of debentures.

(e)   In restricted circumstances, to write-off the premium on the redemption of shares.

(f)   To make a bonus issue.

Allotment at a discount (s580 CA2006)

Neither a private company nor a public company can issue shares at a discount to nominal value.

Payment for shares

Shares may be issued for cash or non-cash consideration (property, know-how, services, etc.).

Minimum payment (s586 CA2006)

Shares issued by a plc must be paid up to the extent of one quarter of the nominal value plus the whole of the premium: s586 CA2006. (This does not apply to shares allotted under an employee share scheme.) Breach of the above rules has the following consequences.

(a)   The shares are treated as if one quarter of its nominal value had been paid.

(b)   The allottee must pay the deficiency in cash with interest.

CAPITAL MAINTENANCE

Serious loss of capital in plcs

The creditors buffer

When members contribute capital to their company, it forms what is known as the 'creditors buffer', that is a pool of funds on which creditors can draw if the company goes into liquidation.

A particular problem in this context is what the CA2006 calls a serious loss of capital in a public company. This arises when net assets are 50 per cent or less of a plc's called up share capital: s656 CA2006. Consider the following balance sheet.

	£m
Fixed assets	1
Net current assets	2
	───
Net assets	3
	───
Share capital	6
Profit and loss account	(3)
	───
	3
	───

On becoming aware of this situation, directors have 28 days to call a General Meeting to consider what steps are to be taken.

The meeting must be held within 56 days of the directors becoming aware of the position. In the event of default, directors are liable to a fine.

Private companies are not required to do this because they have fewer members.

Capital reduction

Under s641 CA2006 a company can buy back or otherwise reduce its share capital. However, three authorities are required for this procedure:

(a)   the power must exist in the Articles;

(b)   a special resolution must be passed; and

(c)   the sanction of the court must be obtained.

However, private companies need not obtain court approval for capital reduction under the CA2006.

If the reduction affects the creditors' buffer then their consent too is required. S135 suggests three circumstances when capital may be reduced.

(a)   to cancel future calls on unpaid capital;

(b)   to write-off share capital that is permanently lost;

(c)   to repay capital in excess of the company's requirements.

In (1) and (2) above, creditors may object to the reduction but not under (3), since the reduction will represent the true value of the company.

Redemption or purchase of own shares

S658 CA2006 provides that companies are not permitted to purchase their own shares and a company cannot be a shareholder of itself (*Trevor v Whitworth* 1887).

However, a company can acquire its own shares by gift, as a result of a court order or where redeemable shares have been issued. Also, a company can purchase its own shares so long as it satisfies the appropriate statutory procedure.

Where a company does acquire its own shares, they must be cancelled or transferred on within a set time period.

Financial assistance for the acquisition of shares

Financial assistance means the company lending money, or guaranteeing a loan made by a third party, to someone to enable that party to buy the company's shares.

It is illegal for a public company or any of its subsidiaries directly or indirectly to provide financial assistance of any sort for the acquisition of shares in itself or its holding company: s's678 and 679.

The following consequences arise if s's678 and 679 is breached.

(a)   The financial assistance (e.g. the guarantee) is void;

(b)   Officers responsible are guilty of a criminal offence;

(c)   Officers of the company in breach of duty are liable to account for any loss suffered by the company as a result.

General exceptions to s678

The rule in s678 does not apply in any of the following circumstances.

(a)   If financial assistance is not the principle purpose of the transaction for the acquisition of shares (e.g. as part of a reconstruction);

(b)   If the purpose of the assistance is the acquisition of own shares but this is an incidental part of a larger purpose of the company (this legalises many management buyouts);

(c)   Where the lending of money is part of the ordinary business of the company;

(d)   It is to or for the benefit of employees.

Private companies

Prior to the introduction of the CA2006 private companies were prohibited from providing financial assistance unless a procedure established in statute was followed. This prohibition effecting private companies has now been removed.

Profits available for distribution

Dividends may not be paid out of capital.

S830 CA2006 states that profits available for distribution are the aggregate of accumulated realised profits less accumulated realised losses.

Realised profits and losses

Realised profit means realised in accordance with accepted accounting principles in force at the accounting date, of which the most important are the four accounting concepts in SSAP 2.

Realised losses include sums written off to provisions (e.g. bad debts expense, provision for depreciation of fixed assets, provision for obsolete stock).

Unrealised profits and losses

An unrealised profit arises on the revaluation of fixed assets upwards (the profit would be realised if the assets were sold at the revalued price).

Additional restrictions on plcs

A public company may not make a distribution if the effect would be to reduce its net assets below the aggregate of called up share capital plus distributable reserves.

Consequences of an excessive distribution

A member is liable to repay a distribution he has received if he knew, or had reasonable grounds to believe, that it was being paid in contravention of the Acts. Where the dividends cannot be recovered from members, every director who was knowingly a party to the unlawful distribution must pay the company the amount lost plus interest.

LOAN CAPITAL

Types of debenture

In addition to capital raised by the issue of shares, companies may need to borrow. This may be achieved by issuing debentures.

A debenture is a document by which a company acknowledges its indebtedness for a loan. To ensure that the debenture holders are adequately protected, the debenture loan is usually secured by a charge, which may be either fixed or floating.

Fixed charges

The charge relates to a specific asset which may be realised by debenture holders to repay their loan (e.g. land, buildings and fixed plant and machinery). Also the value of the charge is fixed and the charge takes priority over all other creditors. Any amount of loan not satisfied by selling the charged asset will rank as an unsecured creditor.

Floating charges

These are created only by incorporated associations. A floating charge is a charge secured on the company's assets generally (i.e. on present and future assets of the company) or of a generic type (e.g. stock in trade). The company can deal with the charged property in the ordinary course of business until some event occurs which causes the charge to become crystallised and fixed. Debts secured by floating charges are repaid after fixed charges and after preferential creditors.

Crystallisation

This is the process by which the floating charge ceases to float over the assets and instead becomes attached to the assets. This occurs in the following circumstances:

(a)   when the company defaults on the debenture agreement;

(b)   when winding up commences;

(c)   when the company ceases business.

In such circumstances the company can no longer deal with any assets subject to the charge.

Remedies for a debenture holder

An unsecured debenture holder ranks as an ordinary trade creditor.

A secured creditor enjoys two remedies in addition to those of an unsecured creditor:

1   selling the charged property to recover the debt; or

2   usually a receiver or administrative receiver is appointed to sell the assets on behalf of debenture holders.

PRIORITY OF CHARGES

If there are different charges over the same property, it will be necessary to ascertain their rankings.

(a)   similar charges rank in order of creation;

(b)   floating charges rank behind fixed charges even if the fixed charges were created later;

(c)   floating charges rank behind preferential creditors.

REGISTRATION OF CHARGES

Particulars of all charges must be registered with the Registrar of Companies within 21 days. Failure to register renders the charge void against the liquidator and any person who acquires an interest in property subject to the charge and the company and its officers may be fined. The charge, therefore, remains valid but unsecured. A debenture holder can register the charge if it appears that the company is unlikely to do so and charges can be validly registered outside the 21-day period.

FACTORS AFFECTING A CHARGE'S VALIDITY

A preference is any transaction undertaken with a desire to improve a creditor's position on a winding up. This will be rendered invalid if it had been given within 6 months of liquidation (2 years if in favour of a connected person).

Floating charges created within 12 months of insolvency (two years if in favour of a connected person) will be rendered invalid if:

(a)   the company was insolvent when the charge was created and

(b)   no consideration was given in exchange for the charge.

SHARES AND DEBENTURES COMPARED

Shares	*Debentures*
Shareholders are members	Debenture holders are creditors
A shareholder has an interest in the company	A debenture holder has a claim against the company
Usually the shareholder can vote at the company's general meeting	No right to vote at the company's general meeting, but has the right to appoint a receiver
Receives a dividend if declared	Receives interest. Always entitled to his interest, can sue for arrears if not paid
Receives the surplus on a winding up after claims of creditors including debenture holders	Receives only the amount of debt owed; takes priority over shareholders in the event of winding up
Shares are capital and the introduction and withdrawal of capital is strictly controlled by the capital maintenance rules	None of the capital maintenance rules apply
Cannot be issued at a discount	May be issued at a discount
Shareholders' dividends are appropriations of profit	Debenture holders' interest is a charge against profit

COMPANY MANAGEMENT — DIRECTORS

Appointment of directors

The CA2006 s250 defines a director as 'any person occupying the position of director by whatever name called'. The test is really one of function: if someone takes part in making decisions by attending meetings of the board then he is a director.

A private company must have at least one director, for a public company the minimum is two directors.

First directors are appointed on incorporation, simply by being named on Form 10. Subsequently, directors are appointed in accordance with the articles, by an ordinary resolution of members in general meeting.

Eligibility for office

The following persons are not eligible to be appointed as directors.

(a)   Persons named in the articles;

(b)   Undischarged bankrupts;

(c)   Anyone over 70 (plc only) (unless permitted by the articles);

(d)   A person who does not meet the shareholding requirements (if any);

(e)   Persons disqualified by the Company Directors Disqualification Act 1986:
- for fraudulent and wrongful trading
- for persistent default in filing returns
- for conviction of a serious indictable offence relating to a company
- for unfitness.

The CA2006 provides that directors must be at least 16 years of age. Any existing director under this age who was appointed prior to the CA2006 will cease to act in this capacity.

Remuneration

Directors' remuneration will be set out in the articles and/or separate contracts.

Payment can be challenged if it is not a genuine payment.

Payment of an unreasonable amount may be classed as a gift: *Re Halt Garage Limited* 1964.

Vacation of office

Retirement by rotation

Table A states that at the first AGM all directors shall retire, and at subsequent AGMs one-third of the board shall retire on a first-in-first-out basis. Retiring directors are eligible for re-election.

Resignation

A director may resign either by notice in writing given to the company or by not offering himself for re-election.

Removal (s168 CA2006)

Removal of a director requires an ordinary resolution (i.e. a simple majority).

Special notice of the resolution must be given by a member to the company, 28 days before the meeting.

The director may make written representations. The director has a right to speak at the meeting.

If a director is removed before the expiry of a fixed-term contract, he may sue the company for breach of contract: *Southern Foundries v Shirlaw* 1940.

Compensation for loss of office (s's215 – 217 CA2006)

Any payment made to a director in connection with his loss of office or retirement requires approval by the members to be lawful (e.g. golden handshakes) unless it is in respect of contractual obligations.

Power of directors

The company's powers are exercised by two bodies: the directors and the members. The extent of directors' powers is generally defined by the articles, the objects clause and the directors' service contracts.

If the directors exceed their powers, or exercise them improperly, their acts can nevertheless be ratified by an ordinary resolution provided the transaction was intra vires (i.e. within the company's powers): *Bamford v Bamford* 1970.

Board meeting

The powers delegated to directors are exercised collectively by voting at board meetings. In the event of equal voting the chairman has the casting vote.

Provided the directors act within their powers the members cannot overturn decisions of the board. But shareholders dissatisfied with directors' policies may seek to:

(a)   remove the directors under s303 CA85;

(b)   regulate their future conduct by altering articles.

Managing director

A managing director may be appointed by the other directors if the articles permit. His powers and duties depend on his service contract. Managing directors are not normally subject to retirement by rotation, but the appointment is automatically terminated if he ceases to be a director: *Southern Foundries v Shirlaw* 1926.

DUTIES OF DIRECTORS

General duties

Duties owed by directors that were formerly found in common law and equity are now codified in the CA2006. Prior to the introduction of this legislation, the primary duty was to act bona fide for the benefit of the company as a whole. The directors had to demonstrate the skill and care of a reasonable man looking after his own affairs. The issue of care and skill was considered in: *Re City Equitable Fire Insurance Company* 1925, where the court laid down three principles:

1   The required degree of skill is what can reasonably be expected from a person of his knowledge and experience.

2   The director does not have to give continuous attention to the affairs of the company but should attend meetings whenever he is reasonably able to do so.

3   A director is justified in trusting an official to perform delegated duties honestly, provided there are no grounds for suspicion and such delegation is permitted by the articles.

The courts realised that looking to what could reasonably be expected of an individual based on knowledge and experience was too low a standard. In consequence, an objective and subjective approach was adopted. This has now been supported under s174 CA2006 which requires directors to 'exercise reasonable care, skill and diligence'. s174(2) further provides that the general knowledge, skill and experience is that reasonably expected of a person carrying out the duties and also that specifically attributed to the individual.

Fiduciary duties

A director is in a position of trust, being in control of the company's assets. This gives rise to certain fiduciary duties.

Beyond the duty of care under s174, other general duties of directors are found in s's171-177 CA2006.

s171 requires directors to act in accordance with the company's constitution and for the purposes from which they are given.

s172 identifies a need for good faith on the part of directors. A duty to promote the success of the company is established in the section. Further, examples of what the director must have regard to are identified. These include employees, suppliers, customers, the community and the environment. The long-term consequences of decisions must be considered with a need to act fairly as between members established. Directors must also have regard to the desirability of maintaining a reputation for high standards in business conduct.

s173 identifies a duty to exercise independent judgment.

s175 contains material on the need to avoid conflict of interest, which is a long-standing feature of the fiduciary duties that attach.

s176 likewise puts in statutory form the duty not to accept benefits from third parties, which again is of long standing.

To satisfy the fiduciary duties now, just as prior to the CA2006 a director needs:

(a)   To act in good faith;

(b)   To use his powers for a proper purpose;

(c)   Not to fetter his discretion. Directors cannot do deals with each other or with outsiders on the way in which they will vote at board meetings;

(d)   To avoid a conflict of interest: *Cook v Deeks* 1916 (depriving the company of assets); *IDC v Cooley* 1972 (resigning to take advantage of an opportunity arising as a result of their directorship).

Statutory duties

The following statutory duties were established under legislation prior to the CA2006, but this Act maintains the relevant duties to reduce the risk of a conflict of interest and because of the past abuses by directors.

(a)   Duty towards employees (now s172 CA2006, formerly in s309 CA85). The directors must have regard to the interests of the company's employees as well as the interests of members.

(b)   Disclosure of interest in contracts (now s177 CA2006, formerly in s317 CA85).

(c)   Substantial property transactions (now in s's190 and 191, formerly in s320 CA85). Any transaction between the company and a director involving a substantial asset (worth more than the lower of £100,000 or 10 per cent of the company's net assets) requires prior approval in a general meeting.

Loans to directors (s197 CA2006)

There is a general prohibition under s197 preventing a company from:

(a)   making a loan to a director;

(b)   entering into a guarantee on behalf of a director;

(c)   providing any security in connection with a loan to a director.

However, there are numerous exceptions to s197, the following loans being valid:

(a)   Loans to directors for any purpose under £10,000;

(b)   Loans to directors to perform their duties, provided that prior approval is given by members;

(c)   Loans by money-lending companies in the ordinary course of business on terms not more favourable than to others.

Relief from liability

In some cases, directors may be relieved from liability for breach of fiduciary duty by resolution of the members in a general meeting.

MINORITY MEMBERS' RIGHTS

The principle of majority control is often referred to as the rule in *Foss v Harbottle*: the company acts according to the will of the majority.

In this case, Foss brought an action against directors who are alleged to have misapplied company property. His action failed as the company was the victim and if it was unwilling to complain the plaintiff has no rights.

The rule therefore recognises

(a)   that decisions made or ratified by the majority cannot be disputed by the minority;

(b)   that directors owe a duty to the company and not to individual members.

DERIVATIVE ACTIONS

A statutory derivative claim can be brought by a member under s260 CA2006. The right to bring the action is vested in the company, and the member is seeking relief on behalf of the company. The claim can only be brought under s260(3) in respect of '. . . an actual or proposed act or omission involving negligence, default, breach of duty or breach of trust by a director . . .'. Further, the claimant is required under s261 CA2006 to obtain court permission in order to be able to continue the action.

A minority shareholder may wish to withdraw his capital by liquidating the company. This is possible under s122 Insolvency Act 1986. However, the following petitions have been successful:

(a)   Failure of the main object (Re *German Date Coffee Company* 1882);

(b)   Where there is management deadlock in the running of the business (Re *Yenidje Tobacco Company* 1916);

(c)   Where the practitioner has been expelled from office as director (*Ebrahimi v Westbourne Galleries* 1973).

A more usual remedy available to dissatisfied minorities is that provided by s994 CA2006 (relief from unfairly prejudicial conduct).

A claim under s994 CA2006 must relate to company affairs that affect the '... interests of members generally or of some part of its members . . .'. S996 CA2006 identifies remedies available with a s994 action and gives the court a wide discretion. Included is the right to make an order regulating the affairs of the company, and further requiring the shares of the claimant to be purchased.

Examples of other minority rights

(a)   10 per cent can require the directors to convene a GM;

(b)   5 per cent or 100 members can require a resolution to be included on the agenda of an AGM;

(c)   15 per cent can object to an alteration of the objects;

(d)   Any member of a private company can prevent an elective or written resolution;

(e)   If no AGM is called, any member can inform the Department of Trade and Industry;

(f)   5 per cent or 50 members can object to conversion of a plc to a private company;

(g)   Any member can prevent conversion from a private limited company to a private unlimited company;

(h)   Representative actions established as exceptions to the *Foss v Harbottle* rule when the minority seek to enforce personal rights;

(i)   Derivative actions established as exceptions to the *Foss v Harbottle* rule where e.g. fraud, illegality or non-compliance with statute is the basis of the action.

The company secretary

Every public company must have a company secretary. A sole director cannot act as a secretary.

The company secretary is the chief administrative officer of the company and can bind the company to the extent of his actual (express or implied) authority. This usually extends only to contracts of an administrative nature: *Panorama Developments Limited v Fidelis Furnishing Fabrics Limited* 1971.

Therefore, the secretary's authority does not extend to:

(a)   making trading contract;

(b)   borrowing money on behalf of the company;

(c)   taking or defending legal proceedings in the company's name.

A company secretary has the following duties.

(a)   Ensuring the company's documents are in order (e.g. returns made to the Registrar);

(b)   Taking minutes of meetings;

(c)   Sending notices to members;

(d)   Countersigning documents to which the company seal, if it has one, is affixed.

11

(a)   Anyone under the age of 15/16/18/20 (1 mark) cannot act as a director of a company. Directors must retire by rotation every .... (1 word) year. A director can be removed on the passing of a/an .... (1 word) resolution. However, ... (2 words) of the resolution must be given.

(3 marks)

(b)   A director owes fiduciary duties to the company which involves the use of powers for a .... (2 words) and also the avoidance of a .... (3 words).   **(2 marks)**

(Total: 5 marks)

12

(a)   The process by which a floating charge becomes a fixed charge is known as .... (1 word). Debentures are usually secured by a .... (1 word).

(2 marks)

(b)   Charges must be registered with the Registrar of Companies within 10/14/21 days The debenture holder is a .... (1 word) of the company.   **(2 marks)**

(c)   A company can deal with its property in the ordinary course of business even though that property is subject to a charge so long as it is a .... (1 word) charge. Capital maintenance rules do/do not apply to debenture holders.   **(2 marks)**

(Total: 6 marks)

13

    (a)   Private companies can/cannot provide financial assistance for the acquisition of their shares. The provision of financial assistance by a public company is a ……………… ……………… (2 words). **(2 marks)**

    (b)   Companies are not permitted to acquire their own shares; however, acquisition will result after the issuing of ……………… ……………… (2 words). Further, in consequence of a ……………… ……………… (2 words), a company acquisition of its shares must take place. **(4 marks)**

                                                                (Total: 6 marks)

14

    (a)   Any member of a company can bring an action under s994 CA2006 on the basis of ……………… ……………… ……………… (3 words). An individual member can also bring a ……………… (1 word) action to enforce a personal entitlement. At common law, actions could be brought under exceptions to the rule in the case of ……………… v ……………….. **(3 marks)**

    (b)   A minority of members of at least 5%/10%/15%/20% can require directors to convene a General Meeting, whilst a minimum 5%, 10%, 15% and 20% members can demand a resolution be added at an Annual General Meeting. **(2 marks)**

    (c)   A private company need not comply with the requirement for the annual appointment of ……………… (1 word). Shorter notice than the required 14 days for a General meeting of a private company will be valid where a minimum 75%, 80%, 90% and 95% of the members with voting rights agree. **(2 marks)**

                                                               (Total: 7 marks)

ETHICS AND BUSINESS

WHY ETHICS ARE VITAL TO ACCOUNTING

Society expects professional accountants to behave and act in the public interest. Behaving ethically in compliance with the *CIMA Code of Practice,* as well as with relevant laws and regulations is an important technical competence. However, underlying compliance is the need for appropriate professional values to underpin decision-making and practice.

An understanding and application of *Professional Values* ensures that the right decisions are made when challenges to professionalism and ethics raise themselves in everyday practice.

Working practices that are informed by *Ethical Principles* are likely to minimise the chances of professional problems arising and to provide early warning of potentially compromising situations.

While the purpose of both values and principles is *to protect the public at large* from the consequence of bad accounting practice, working with them is likely to spare the accountant career-threatening experiences!

THE ROLE OF PROFESSIONAL REGULATORS

The Financial Reporting Council aims to ensure that all corporate bodies are clear and transparent in the way that they report financial dealings. Sound accounting practices and compliance with best professional and ethical practice are promoted and assured by the Professional Oversight Body for Accounting and the Auditing Practices Board. They educate, regulate and police the standards set down nationally. These, in turn, reflect the relevant international standards laid down by the International Federation of Accountants, upon whose Code of Ethics the CIMA Code is based.

THE PRINCIPLES OF PUBLIC LIFE

Public Sector Accountants need to comply with the Seven Principles of Public Life, but they nonetheless provide useful guidance to all accountants, since accounting is there to instil public confidence in the integrity of financial accounting. The Principles set out by the Committee for Standards in Public Life are Selflessness and Integrity; Objectivity and Accountability; Openness, Honesty and Leadership.

THE IMPORTANCE OF INDIVIDUAL VALUES, AS OPPOSED TO JUST RULES

Values in Accounting move the focus of activity from merely going through the process correctly, to ensuring that there can be trust in financial accounting because the practices underpinning accounting and the people undertaking tasks can be *trusted,* can be demonstrated to be *reliable,* can be shown to work to the *highest standards* and are seen to *work for the good of the stakeholders and the public at large.* On an individual level, these are manifested by understanding and putting into practice ethical standards.

THE IMPORTANCE OF CORPORATE RESPONSIBILITY

On a corporate level, these are demonstrated by having systems to support professionalism and report professional wrongdoing, while actively monitoring how the company, in its own right, affects society around it. The impact of the company on the community, the environment, its workforce and its clients is assessed, managed and explained to its stakeholders through means such as Corporate Responsibility Policies and Corporate Responsibility Reports.

PLAYING BY THE RULES AND BEING A REAL PROFESSIONAL

Of course, we have to comply with the rules. However, rules tend to be all or nothing and, so often in private life we might just do enough *to comply with the rules* and take advantage of ambiguous interpretations to 'bend' them to our advantage. The values-based approach to Ethics encourages us to strive to do the right thing in our public roles, even if it means going further than the rules strictly require us to go.

Obviously, given that the *values strive for best professional practice* and rules are set at the minimum acceptable practice, a person who pursues what is right will never stop short of complying with the legislative and regulatory framework. However, a person who merely ticks the boxes or technically complies with the rules can still end up collapsing a company or at the heart of a huge financial scandal!

THE SEVEN PRINCIPLES OF PUBLIC LIFE

The 'Principles' were issued by the 'Committee of Standards in Public Life'. They effectively reflect the professional standards of accountants.

The Principles are:

Selflessness – not look for personal gain, but rather that which is in the public interest.

Integrity – those in public office should not place themselves in a position where outside factors are an influence on performance of official duties.

Objectivity – awards of e.g. contracts or benefits should be based on merit.

Accountability – acknowledge work and decision making will be open to scrutiny.

Openness – accept the need to have available, or make available information of work done, decisions made and reasons for decisions. Any restrictions on disclosure or availability of information should be based on the needs of public interest.

Honesty – recognise a need to declare any private interests relevant and work to protect the public interest.

Leadership – support and promote in the broad sense the principles. An obligation attaches to management accountants to go beyond merely complying with rules. A framework approach is recognised where accountants 'self-regulate'. This is aimed towards the encouragement of trust and confidence. Standards and culture within a company will be measured by identified ethical values.

The values of a company can be linked to its business practice and the expectation levels of outsiders.

Professional accounting bodies, in establishing an ethics code, provide a foundation for the positive ethical direction encouraged and reinforce the cultural expectations.

PERSONAL QUALITIES – 3 RS AND T & C

The accountant is judged personally on their professionalism; by the client, the regulator or the employer. Personal qualities that demonstrate a sense of professionalism in dealings with others and which inform the right way to go about work are the 3 Rs:

*R*eliability – the idea that an accountant will do what they have said they will do and what can be reasonably expected of them;

*R*esponsibility – that they will take it upon themselves to do what needs to be done and answer for their mistakes if necessary;

*R*espect – that they will treat others with dignity and seek to understand their cultural and personal expectations in the way they are treated.

*T*imely & *C*ourteous follow naturally on from reliability and respect. The professional is always *timely,* not merely when it is required for business efficacy and *courteous,* not merely when it is needed for good corporate relations.

ETHICAL PRINCIPLES – COPPI

The ethical principles that engender trust and that should always be in the forefront of decision-making when deciding how and whether to act can be summarised by the following:

*C*onfidentiality – thinking before opening one's mouth, writing a message or listening to someone, so that you ask yourself:

'Is this my information to give out?', or 'Is this information I have permission to give out?', or 'Is this information I am supposed to receive?', or

'Should I disclose this information because I have a legal duty to do so?', or 'Should I disclose this information to assist in the regulation and review of professional standards?'

Objectivity – thinking, when embarking on a decision, so that you ask yourself, 'How ought I to deal with this in best practice as a professional?' as opposed to 'How do I want to deal with this/how does my client want me to deal with this?' Often the answer could or should be the same, but if it is not, then professional standards should prevail.

Professional Competence and Care – knowing *what* you ought to do in best professional practice, including the standard of care required to be complied with for the task shows that you comply with the standards required by professional rules and applicable law.

Professional Behaviour – knowing *how* you ought to perform your tasks and what other things you should do to ensure that you promote trust and confidence in the profession, according to professional standards and through the demonstration of personal qualities.

Integrity – acting always in a way that makes you feel and those around believe that you make sound, impartial judgements, that are in the interests of the client, your employer and public at large and when you cannot because of a conflict, you take the responsibility to ensure that the conflict is brought to the attention of an authority that can resolve it in an ethical way.

PROFESSIONAL ATTRIBUTES – IAS

For accountants and accountancy to have continued value in ensuring that Public and Private Financial management is *accountable,* it is vital that the profession as a whole and each of its members is seen to have the attributes of Independence, Accountability and a commitment to Social Responsibility.

Independence – Accounting seeks to explain on a commonly understood basis how finance is being managed, so that businesses, public bodies and individuals can deal with each other with some measure of confidence in the financial security and reliability of their partners. In order to ensure that this is possible, there must be confidence that professionals can be *trusted to be independent* and that they behave in a manner that is *beyond the suspicion of bias or influence.*

Accountability – The profession and professionals need to be *up front with what they do, why they do it and how they do it.* Regulation and transparency assist in this process, as does striving to explain the what's, how's and why's, rather than waiting to be asked.

Social Responsibility – Accounting exists to ensure that the private financial arrangements of public and private sector bodies integrate with their role and place within society.

Therefore the accountant, although providing a paid-for service to the client, does so on behalf of the community at large, rather than merely for private gain.

The accountant owes their existence to social need and therefore should *always be conscious of how their own actions might have a social impact,* not only on obvious stakeholders, such as the client and employer, but also on the profession, the public at large and the community within which they work.

Where there are apparent tensions, the professional should seek ways to work in partnership to alleviate any negative impact of their work or seek guidance from, or feedback to, professional bodies that may be able to make a difference.

THE REGULATORY FRAMEWORK FOR ETHICS

Accounting exists within an international community and for this reason, common standards apply internationally. However, different countries have different expectations of their professions. For this reason, the standards set for the UK by bodies such as CIMA may go further than the *International Financial Accounting Committee Code of Practice.*

Professional ethics in this country are led not only by the professional bodies, but also by legal obligations set by Parliament, by Government Departments (through Regulations etc) and by decisions of the courts about the scope of the *Law.* Sometimes these changes can be very swift and very specific, overriding or adding to the standards set down by the CIMA Code of Practice and invariably raising the standards expected of the profession.

The *CIMA Code of Practice* aims to reflect the minimum standards set out both internationally and through national law, while providing further guidance relevant to UK professional practice outside the remit of the international accounting fraternity or of the law makers.

On occasion, where there is a sudden, unexpected change in the law, Legal Requirements may temporarily exceed the standards laid down by the Code of Practice. It is for this reason that you should keep *continually updating your knowledge of professional standards.*

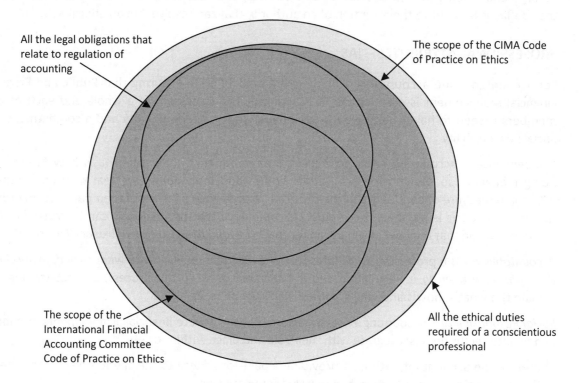

All the legal obligations that relate to regulation of accounting

The scope of the CIMA Code of Practice on Ethics

The scope of the International Financial Accounting Committee Code of Practice on Ethics

All the ethical duties required of a conscientious professional

The relationship between different ethical regulatory frameworks

ETHICAL CONFLICT

ETHICAL PROBLEM-SOLVING

Saying what a professional should do is one thing, but doing it is something else. At different levels, the balance between public and private interest, between ethics and business efficacy is made by continual application of review, appraisal, judgement, consultation, action and, again, review. Managing ethical issues is a dynamic process that needs to be constantly undertaken and updated in line with new information. Neither at the level of the professional body, nor at the corporate level is there any guarantee that professionals will act in accordance with professional ethics. Ultimately, it is the individual's responsibility. Moreover, organisations struggle to balance what they want to do with what they ought, ethically to do

The *profession* itself has pressures on it to limit the extent of regulation and compliance because of the bureaucracy that it encourages in companies, the burden it places on membership and the resultant cost it passes onto clients. On the other hand, the public and the government expect close regulation of accounting and each financial scandal sees calls for tighter regulation. A professional body like CIMA is pulled two ways; it can either trust in the professionalism of companies or it can closely control standards through detailed regulation and inspection. **Law and Regulation** framework draws the boundaries of what must be done, but consultation and continual review are the only means by which ethical standards can help make the right balance.

For example in 2005, CIMA:

1   *Reviewed* the current practices and problems within the profession, nationally and inter nationally;

2   *Appraised* the framework in place to see whether it adequately dealt with problems arising from practice and supported members in doing the right thing for the profession, the public at large and their business stakeholders;

3   *Judged* that as a regulator it had a duty to provide better and more complete guidance on ethical issues through a Code of Practice on Ethics;

4   *Consulted* on the content, detail and proposed approach, making reference to existing frameworks and legislation nationally and internationally;

5   *Acted* to make the Code known and to provide the support through education, help and guidance;

6   Are committed to *ongoing review* of the relevance and effectiveness of the Code.

Corporate entities are similarly drawn in different directions. The desires of the shareholders and clients might pull in different directions from the wishes of employees, the needs of the general public and what is best for the communities which their business has an impact upon. *Corporate Governance Standards* that ensure the company is directed to consider all of the relevant matters is complemented by *Corporate Social Responsibility* initiatives which aim to provide balance to the impact of business on communities or to give something back. Transparency, openness in governance and partnership working with the regulators, public bodies and other stakeholders can help a business steer between meeting the needs of the shareholders and its broader social obligations.

For example, companies:

1   *Review* their activities against their corporate plans in line with policies set down for the environment, diversity and other aspects of corporate social responsibility;

2   *Appraise* whether they are meeting their targets, mission and objectives in relations to these matters;

3   *Judge* whether they need to act to go further to meet these aims and whether there are matters that they are failing to address;

4   *Consult* to get feedback from shareholders, employees and others in lien with their statutory duties and corporate constitution;

5   *Act* to put into place improvements to structures and processes to ensure they fit the plans and values of the organisation;

6   Use the Board and auditors to ensure *ongoing review* of the relevance and effectiveness of the Corporate strategies and plans.

Individual accountants experience pressures from a variety of directions, all of which call on the accountant to do the right thing, by favouring that interest. The following influences can pull a person in several directions:

1   Personal morality;

2   Loyalty to one's family and friends;

3   Sense of obligation to one's sponsors and supporters;

4   Commitment to the team in which one works;

5   Obligation to meet the clients' expectations;

6   Duty of trust and confidence to one's employer;

7   Desire to do the best possible job in the circumstances;

8   Feeling of duty to maintain the good name of the profession;

9   Desire to be open, honest and above reproach;

10   Responsibility to society and the public interest.

None of these pressures are bad things in themselves. In fact the pursuit of each of these things in the appropriate circumstances would be deemed to be virtuous and ethical. But the road to Hell is paved with virtuous and ethical aspirations. It is rare that people breach professional ethics because they want to do bad things, or because they are bad people. People get into ethical difficulties because they wrongly give weight to one of these influences or fail to see where pursuit of one of them brings them in conflict with another.

If we break down these influences, we can see how the more the motivation is aimed at meeting public standards, the more importance it is to be given in ethical thinking. The higher up the scale (8–10), the closer these comply with national and international standards. Following these motivations, rather than motivations in the private or personal sphere (1–5), clearly avoid some of the more significant individual breaches of ethics.

Issues that call on motivations between 4 and 8 often cause the most difficulties, because personal and employment issues become wrapped up together. When there is a conflict between the team, client, employer or regulator and the public duty, we most often feel exposed because the normal support to 'do the right thing' is pulling us in the opposite direction than our public duty.

By reviewing the work that you do on a regular basis, for example, at natural points within a work cycle for ethical compliance, it is often possible to identify possible ethical problems. Ethical problems come in all shapes and sizes, but few have signs to highlight that that is what they are, so you need to ask yourself questions. The following table gives you the range of problems from easy to hard.

ETHICS, LAW, GOVERNANCE AND SOCIAL RESPONSIBILITY

Ethical Codes and Legislation

If an ethical issue arises, the approach may well be 'what is the right thing to do' or 'what is the best thing to do'. The individual has options guided by standards and possibly codes as found with the CIMA Code. Where legislation exists, the individual has the need for choice taken from them. Compliance is required. The CIMA Code provides that the law prevails over any other source or guide that may conflict with the law.

Ethical Codes and Contracts

Conflict can arise where an individual is required to act in a certain way in the course of their employment. Where breach of professional ethics and breach of contract conflict, the profession of the individual should take priority over the employer. A dilemma may arise whereby the loss of a clients business may be the possible consequence of following ethical demands. Employment Tribunals and the courts ultimately may be the arbiters of conduct. Equally, the law does offer clear general guidance in e.g. refusing to support conduct in breach of public policy. Also, professional bodies e.g. CIMA offer support for the individual where conflict with the employer through contract exists. This can be seen in preventing unprofessional conduct through the imposition of personal liability.

Corporate Governance and Social Responsibility

Social responsibility can be a base used by an individual where conflict with employer wishes arises. It can assist the identified desire to achieve ethical standards necessary. This applies where the relationship between the organisation and outside community is considered. Governance highlights the generic way in which a company or other organisation is run. Organisational responsibility to stakeholders is often identified with policies on social responsibility. The need for such policies exists to show good governance. A need to support the ethical codes of professions arises through governance and recognition of social responsibility.

What is the problem?	*What am I looking for?*	*How do I deal with it?*	*Where do I seek guidance?*
Failure to meet professional standards – this is simple non-compliance with rules and standards	Is this to the standard of work/client care/professionalism expected of a competent accountant?	• Check your facts and review the available information. • Check the Codes, Law and latest professional updates to see whether there is a genuine problem and recommended solution. • Check the systems in place in your institutions to deal with this and make use of them. In addition, you may need to • Ensure that you declare any underperformance to manager or, if appropriate corporate compliance officer or regulator (respecting confidentiality).	• Line manager • Compliance/legal department • CIMA
Compliance with professional rules, but falling short of the expected professional behaviour or values – this is failure to live up to the professional expectations that go beyond the minimum standards expected of accountants	Are these actions in line with the values of the profession and will these maintain and enhance the standing of myself, my company and my profession?	• Check your facts and review the available information. • Check the Codes, Law and latest professional updates to see whether there is a genuine problems and recommended solution. • Check the systems in place in your institutions to deal with this and make use of them. • Improve performance	• Line manager • CIMA

What is the problem?	What am I looking for?	How do I deal with it?	Where do I seek guidance?
		In addition, you may need to • Seek a second opinion from a reliable source about your standards of professionalism (you may be being too hard on yourself! But ensure you respect confidentiality). • Confront pressures that may be forcing you to perform at the minimum standards • Seek guidance and support to improve performance.	• Line manager • Compliance/ legal department • CIMA
Conflict of interest – this is where you identify that you are in a position where you may have obligations to more than party whose interests have the potential, however remove in the future, to be incompatible.	Would continuing with this work mean that there is a possibility that I might have a professional obligation to one party/client that would be to the detriment of another party/ client that would be to the detriment of another party/client to whom I owe an obligation?	• Check your facts and review the available information • Check the Codes, Law and latest professional updates to see whether there is a genuine problem and recommended solution. • Check the processes in your organisation addressing/preventing conflicts of interest for to ensure that you have complied, but also that there are adequate safeguards to prevent the same arising. In addition, you may need to • Declare the interests of both parties as soon as you realise it (respecting confidentiality) • Cease to work for one or other party (sometimes both), ensuring that they are not prejudiced unduly by the change in their status. • Keep and maintain full documentation of anything you do.	• Line manager • Compliance/ legal department • CIMA

What is the problem?	What am I looking for?	How do I deal with it?	Where do I seek guidance?
Ethical dilemma – this is where there are only limited courses of action, each of which is likely to breach an ethical duty and where not acting is not an option.	Am I being called upon to perform a duty for one party that means I would fail in performance of a duty to another party?	• Check your facts and review the available information. • Check the Codes, Law and latest professional updates to see whether there is a genuine problem and recommended solution. • Check the systems in place in your institutions to deal with this and make use of them. • Notify your manager or/and, if appropriate, compliance/legal department or even regulatory body if there is a problem. In addition, you may need to • Declare to parties to whom you owe a duty you consider to be the conflicting problem what (respecting confidentiality) • Identify whether you owe a higher duty e.g. public, as opposed to personal duty, and comply with that • Seek to minimise the scope of the damage to others as soon as you become aware of the problem • Keep and maintain full documentation of anything you do • Don't panic, being ain an ethical dilemma is not a crime – not dealing with it might be.	• Line manager • Compliance/legal department • Board of Directors • Audit Committee • CIMA

CORPORATE GOVERNANCE

THE DEFINITION OF CORPORATE GOVERNANCE

'Corporate governance' has not been defined by legislation or the courts. The definition provided by the Cadbury Committee provides that it is 'the system by which companies are directed and controlled'. The term relates primarily to the management of public listed companies, and particularly the control, business efficacy and accountability of the management. Corporate governance does apply to a lesser extent to private companies. What has come to be regarded as corporate governance is contained in the 'Combined Code'. Under the Code merely a disclosure obligation exists in that UK listed companies must merely identify in their Annual Reports that they have complied with the Code. The Code does not have the force of law and so compliance is voluntary. To have a compulsory requirement, whilst not desired, might be the consequence of widespread non-compliance now.

THE INTERACTION OF CORPORATE GOVERNANCE WITH BUSINESS ETHICS AND COMPANY LAW

Overlap exists between corporate governance, business ethics and company law. In relation to company law, this can be seen in that directors owe a fiduciary duty to the members, they must always act in good faith and in the best interests of the company. Directors must not obtain secret profits and must not allow personal interests to conflict with the best interests of the company.

The law provides for the internal regulation of director activities, and the CA2006 provides for the removal of directors for any reason with a majority vote by the members.

Whilst the law may address the issue of director conduct and standards; those who invest in companies may not be inclined to pursue remedies where a director acts improperly. Fund managers invest with a view to achieving capital growth, but usually will have no wish to participate in internal affairs of a company. Further, a company may have hundreds or even thousands of investors and so effective regulation by them of director activities is difficult.

Criminal law addresses ethical behaviour of directors through, for example, the recognition of insider dealing as a criminal offence. Directors and other insiders are prohibited from using inside information for personal benefit. To so benefit is seen as wrong and unethical.

Such conduct is a criminal offence under the Criminal Justice Act 1993. The drafting of relevant legislation and effectiveness of its implementation can show the ongoing need for review and development in order to achieve protection for investors.

Ethics has to be considered in relation to the work of accountants also. Accountants acting as auditors must be independent of the relevant company. However, criticism of this independence has arisen where the relevant accountants have entered into contracts with the same company to carry out other accounting work. Consideration of the accountants financial interests have also been the basis of concern. To address such criticisms, the Auditing Practice Board established auditing standards and guidance.

Corporate governance relates to economics and finance, as well as social and environmental matters.

THE HISTORY OF CORPORATE GOVERNANCE INTERNATIONALLY

The issue of ownership and control was prominent in the historical development of this area. Private companies and the large public companies that trade internationally can clearly be distinguished in this regard. With many private companies the shareholders are also the directors and so ownership and control resides with the same people. It is with the large public companies that the investors ownership is so markedly separated from company control which rests with the board.

In the US and UK, the input of institutional investors has grown dramatically and today they hold about 60% of the shares in public listed companies. Effective control of directors in public companies has been problematic to implement. Significant is the fact that the managers of investment funds may be more likely to sell securities in a company where a problem is seen to exist, rather than become involved in a time-consuming exercise to address director control. Examples have arisen, particularly in America, of directors warding off possible takeover bids, involving consideration of corporate governance issues. The role of the media has contributed in highlighting the need for further development in corporate governance.

Enron provided a good example of how public awareness of corporate governance issues was assisted by media involvement. Also, the facts revealed conduct that showed the need for the control factor to be addressed further in relation to directors and accountants.

Enron's problems arose out of

- Unsustainable growth;
- Requiring increased borrowing;
- Excessive borrowing took place;
- To maintain confidence this had to be hidden;
- A number of subsidiaries were formed to avoid the disclosure of borrowing in the balance sheet.

The directors, chief executives and the auditors were found to be primarily responsible for the collapse of Enron. The effectiveness of corporate governance measures have been brought into question in consequence of the findings in this matter. Guilty pleas have been entered in relation to fraud, insider dealing, money laundering and obstructing justice by destroying relevant documentation. The role of the auditors in conspiring with the directors to avoid disclosure of the borrowing and also the issue of independence were highlighted.

In Europe the need for a common approach rather than a separate code of European corporate governance was seen as appropriate. Through directives the development of controls and establishing of a common approach are developing. Disclosure of financial information, director remuneration and also the role in management of independent nonexecutive directors are areas of development that have emerged. The EU has established an EU Corporate Governance Forum made up of 15 members who have the overall objective of coordinating corporate governance developments within member states.

In the UK, mismanagement of public companies has been seen in a number of instances, for example, with regard to Guinness and also Robert Maxwell. A number of reports relating to corporate governance on public limited companies were introduced in the 1990s.

These included:

The Cadbury Committee Report 1992

This Committee recommended that companies listed on the Stock Exchange should comply with a Code which required:

- The independence of non-executive directors.
- Executive directors should be vetted by a committee made up of non-executive directors.
- A maximum three-year service contract for executive directors.
- Executive directors' remuneration should be determined by a remuneration committee.
- Non-executive directors should be in the majority on an Audit Committee to oversee the company financial matters.
- The same person should not be chief executive and chairman.

The Greenbury Committee Report 1995

This Report contained a further Code. The level of remuneration received by the directors of listed companies became a political embarrassment and the Code to a significant extent addressed this issue. Many, but not all of the recommendations of the Report were incorporated into the Stock Exchange listing rules.

The Hampel Committee Report 1998

This Report added to that already addressed by the two previous committees and related primarily to public listed companies.

Report content highlighted:

- The need for provision of information to executive and non-executive directors of their responsibilities and duties.
- Non-executive directors should make up one-third of the board.
- Executive directors must have appropriate experience.
- Director contracts should not exceed twelve months.
- Remuneration and nomination for director appointment were also dealt with.

The Combined Code, a general code of good practice, based on the Hampel Report was produced by the London Stock Exchange. This did not have the force of law. However, a fine could be imposed by the Stock Exchange for non-compliance.

Subsequent Reports have been the Turnbull Report (1999) which considered the need to look at likely risks facing a company and the need for internal controls, assessment and transparency. Later came the Higgs Report (2003) which followed the Enron collapse. This Report highlighted the importance of collective board responsibility.

The Smith Report on Audit Committees (2003) built on existing good practice and highlighted the importance of auditor independence.

DIRECTOR DUTIES OF SKILL AND CARE AND THE EFFECTS OF CORPORATE GOVERNANCE

Information of the powers of directors can be found in the memorandum of association, articles of association, the shareholder agreement and the individual's service contract.

In relation to the duty of care owed, the courts will have regard to the knowledge and experience of the individual. The degree of skill required is that of a reasonably diligent person, having the knowledge, skill and experience of the individual director. The duty of care generally aligns with the standard of behaviour expected of a director.

Directors also owe fiduciary duties, whereby they should act in the best interests of the company and avoid conflict of interest. These duties are owed primarily to the members as a body. The aims of the law relating to the duty of care and that relating to corporate governance differ significantly. Corporate governance is aimed at the protection of stakeholders and so goes much further than merely the shareholders who have rights on a breach of duty. The duties owed by directors at Common Law now are codified in the Companies Act 2006.

BOARD STRUCTURES

The role of the board and corporate governance

Board structures in the UK

In the UK, companies usually have one board which is responsible for management and governance. This is sometimes referred to as the 'unitary' board.

The unitary board structures can be classified into three groups:

1   The all-executive board. Mainly found in private and subsidiary companies. (All directors have a management role and it appears they monitor their own performance.)

2   The majority executive board. (Made up of executive and non-executive directors.)

3   The majority non-executive board. (Found moreso in public companies. A need exists to clearly separate the role of the director from the role of the executive, and concentrate on corporate governance issues rather than management.)

Board structures in France

1   Unitary board with a combined Chairman and Chief Executive.

2   Unitary board with separate functions of the Chairman and Chief Executive.

3   Two-tier board made up of

Supervisory board

Management committee

Board structure in Germany

In all joint stock companies and most limited liability companies a two-tier board structure is found. As in France there is a Supervisory Board and a Management Board. Both Boards report on corporate governance in the annual report.

Role of the board

It is the responsibility of the board to:

*   Provide leadership of the company;
*   Set the company values and standards;
*   Ensure obligations to shareholders are met;
*   Be responsible for the company policy;
*   Have overall responsibility for management.

REQUIREMENTS OF THE REVISED COMBINED CODE

The main requirements of the Code are:

*   The separation of the role of the Chairman and Managing Director;
*   Independent non-executive directors to participate as board members and provide independent judgement;

- Recruitment of non-executive directors from the legal, financial and public sectors;
- Need to identify matters that require a board decision;
- Need for a competent company secretary;
- The provision of a report along with an annual review relating to internal controls;
- The establishing of board committees;
- All directors and committee members should attend the AGM;
- Encouraging of institutional shareholders to participate to a greater extent in company affairs.

THE REGULATORY GOVERNANCE FRAMEWORK FOR COMPANIES

The regulatory governance framework can be found in legislation, delegated legislation case law and codes.

These include:

- The Companies Act 2006;
- The Company Directors Disqualification Act 1986;
- The Insolvency Act 1986;
- The Financial Services Act 1986;
- The Criminal Justice Act 1993;
- Stock Exchange Listing Requirements 1984;
- Articles of Association;
- The Revised Combined Code 2003;
- The City Code on Takeovers and Mergers;
- Codes of practice established by professional bodies, for example CIMA.

Note also that the Company Law Reform Bill at present going through Parliament contains reforms aimed at addressing shareholder engagement in company affairs and investment culture.

BEST PRACTICE – POLICIES AND PROCEDURE

The Revised Combined Code deals with the most important aspects of best practice for listed companies. The most recent edition was introduced in June 2008. It took effect at the same time as the FSA Corporate Governance rules that implemented EU requirements on audit committees and corporate governance statements.

Principles in the Revised Code are directed towards encouraging members, auditors and non-executive directors to accept their legal responsibilities and oversee company stewardship. Also, introduce suitable checks on executive directors.

The principle areas dealt with in the Revised Combined Code are:

The Board

This should meet regularly. The annual statement should identify how the board functions. Also, power delegated to management should be identified. People with senior roles on the board and/or committees should be identified. Meetings of non-executive directors with the chairman and also meetings with the senior independent director should be held at least once a year. Unresolved concerns should be minute. Written information of any concerns a retiring non-executive director has should be provided to the chairman.

The chairman and chief executive

Chairman and chief executive roles should be clearly identified. The same individual should not act in both roles. Generally a chief executive should not become chairman of the same company.

Board balance and independence

A board should be made up of both executive and non-executive directors. At least half of the board members should be independent non-executive directors. What is meant by 'independent' is identified. This excludes anyone who has served on the board for more than 9 years, anyone who has been a company employee in the previous 5 years or anyone who had a material business relationship in the last 3 years.

Appointment to the board

The appointment process should be begun by a nominations committee. Appointment should be on merit, with consideration given to the availability of the individual. The appointment process should be formal and rigorous. Following amendments made to the Code in 2008, an individual can now be chairman of two FTSE 100 companies.

Information and professional development

On appointment to the board, a director should receive induction. Updating of director skills is a responsibility of the chairman. A competent company secretary should be appointed who is responsible to the board for ensuring compliance with board procedures.

An annual evaluation of the board's performance should take place. The chairman should propose changes on the basis of the evaluation.

Director re-election and remuneration

Every director should be elected by the members at the first AGM after appointment and then every three years. Non-executive directors can serve for more than 9 years, but a lengthy appointment should be subject to rigorous review.

Remuneration should be performance linked. A formal and transparent procedure for the determining of director pay should be established. A remuneration committee should be established that consists of at least 3 members.

Internal control

A system should be established to safeguard company assets and shareholders investments. This system should be annually reviewed. Process for shareholder opinion to be communicated to the board should be established. Institutional shareholders should look to greater participation in company affairs and major shareholders should attend AGMs where possible.

Audit committee

An audit committee should be established that consists of at least 3 independent non-executive directors. This committee is to recommend appointment of an auditor who should be independent.

15

(a)   The Cadbury Committee defined corporate governance as 'the system by which companies are ………………… ………………… ………………… '(3 words).   **(2 marks)**

(b)   Under the Combined Code a ………………… (1 word) obligation exists with compliance with the Code being ………………… (1 word)   **(2 marks)**

(Total: 4 marks)

16

(a)   The unitary board structure in the UK is classified into three groups that are 1…………………, 2 ………………… and 3 …………………   **(3 marks)**

(b)   In France, the board structure includes a two-tier board made up of 1 ………………… and 2 ………………… The unitary board in France is recognised with combined and separate functions of the ………………… (1 word) and ………………… ………………… (2 words).   **(3 marks)**

(Total: 6 marks)

Section 2

OBJECTIVE TEST QUESTIONS

COMPARISON OF ENGLISH LAW WITH ALTERNATIVE LEGAL SYSTEMS

1   While taking driving lessons John drove negligently and injured his instructor. John's duty of care in this case will be

   A   The same as that owed by every driver

   B   That of any unqualified driver

   C   Assessed on the basis of John's specific experience and skill

   D   That which might reasonably be expected of a similarly inexperienced driver

2   In negligence, to prove that damage arose from a breach of duty it must be shown that the breach caused the damage and

   A   The type of injury was reasonably foreseeable

   B   The extent of injury was reasonably foreseeable

   C   The particular injury was reasonably foreseeable

   D   Both the extent and type of injury was reasonably foreseeable

3   What is the effect of the maxim *Res Ipsa Loquitur* (the thing speaks for itself) in connection with the tort of negligence?

   A   There is no need to prove damage

   B   The plaintiff contributed to his own misfortunes

   C   The plaintiff impliedly assented to the act which caused the injury

   D   The burden of proof is placed on the defendant

4   Which of the following does not need to be shown in an action for the tort of negligence?

   A   That a duty of care was owed to the plaintiff by the defendant

   B   That there was breach of that duty of care

   C   That the defendant intended to harm the plaintiff

   D   That injury or damage was caused by the failure to exercise reasonable care

5   Tudor Ltd has three employees: Henry, Edward and Mary. In an argument with a customer over Britain's continued membership of the European Union, Henry assaulted the customer. Whilst driving goods on behalf of the company, Edward drove the company's van negligently. Whilst driving a company car to go on her holidays, Mary picked up a hitch-hiker who was injured as a result of Mary's negligent driving. For which of these acts of its employees will Tudor Ltd be vicariously liable?

A   All of them

B   Those of Edward and Mary

C   That of Edward only

D   Those of Henry and Mary

6   Which of the following statements reflects the position of an occupier of premises as regards his duty to give a warning of danger on the premises?

A   No warning can absolve the occupier for responsibility to lawful visitors to the premises

B   A warning by the occupier may be adequate for adult visitors to the building but not for children

C   A warning by the occupier may be adequate for expert visitors to the building but not for other adults

D   A warning by the occupier will always absolve him from responsibility to lawful visitors to the premises

7   Edna drove her car negligently and mounted the pavement causing injury to Fred, a pedestrian. Fred's injuries were not serious but unfortunately he suffered from a rare blood disease which resulted in his being off work for six months. Fred was a high flying executive and claims for loss of earnings of £60,000. Edna disputes this claim as excessive. What is the position?

A   Edna is only liable for normal damages. Fred's disease is a *novus actus interveniens* and could not be foreseen

B   Edna is liable for full damage since she must take her victim as she finds him

C   Edna will not be liable for full damage. Under the "thin skull" rule, the presence of the serious blood disease could not have been foreseen

D   Edna will be liable only for the damage which could have been foreseen, Fred's loss of earnings were special damages

8   A Parliamentary Bill becomes an Act of Parliament

A   When it passes through the committee stage

B   On receiving its third reading

C   When passed by both Houses of Parliament

D   On receiving the Royal Assent

9   What is the normal burden of proof placed upon the prosecution in a criminal case?

A   Balance of probabilities

B   Beyond every reasonable doubt

C   Beyond any doubt

D   Beyond reasonable doubt

10   Which European Community Law-making measure is applicable to members without any need for legislation?

A   An enactment

B   A decision

C   A regulation

D   A directive

11   Which European Union institution has law-making powers?

A   The Council of Ministers

B   The European Commission

C   The European Parliament

D   The European Court of Justice

12   There is concern over the validity of certain statutory instruments issued by a minister. How can the courts control such delegated legislation?

A   By applying rules of natural justice

B   By determining if it is against public policy

C   By discretionary power to declare void a regulation that is inequitable

D   By use of the doctrine of *ultra vires*

13   Statements made by *obiter dicta* are

A   Binding in certain courts hearing similar disputes

B   Not binding unless made by the House of Lords

C   Principles of law which relate to the facts of the dispute upon which the decision is based

D   Not binding on any later court determining a similar dispute but may be regarded as judicial authority

14   Which of the following is not an example of indirect or delegated legislation?

A   An order in Council

B   A statutory instrument

C   A judicial precedent

D   A bye-law

15   Which of the following statements is untrue?

    A   Decisions of the House of Lords* override statute

    B   Appeals can be made from the House of Lords* to the European Court of Justice

    C   The House of Lords* is not bound by its own previous decisions

    D   Decisions of the House of Lords* bind all lower courts

16   What does the 'Golden Rule' of statutory interpretation mean?

    A   Words should be given their ordinary meaning

    B   The meaning of the words can be gathered from their context

    C   Words should be given the meaning which is likely to give effect to the purpose or reform which the statute intended

    D   Words should be given their ordinary grammatical meaning unless the meaning is manifestly absurd

17   Portuguese law was an influence in the development of law in which one of the following?

    A   Sri Lanka

    B   Malaysia

    C   Hong Kong and Macau

    D   Hong Kong only

* now Supreme Court

THE LAW OF CONTRACT

18   An advertisement to sell a car in a newspaper will amount to

    A   An offer

    B   A mere statement of price

    C   An invitation to treat

    D   A declaration of intent

19   What is the consequence if a contract is void at law?

    A   It is destitute of legal effect

    B   Further performance is excused

    C   The innocent party may repudiate

    D   Either party may repudiate

20 An offer was made by letter posted in London and delivered in Birmingham. A reply was made by fax machine in Manchester and received by the offer's fax machine in Liverpool. Where is the contract made?

A   Where the offer was made in London

B   Where the acceptance was put into the fax machine in Manchester

C   Where the acceptance was received on the fax machine in Liverpool

D   Where the letter making the offer was received in Birmingham

21 In relation to social and domestic agreements the court

A   Assumes the parties did intend to create a legally binding contract

B   Presumes that the parties did not intend to create a legally binding contract

C   Does not consider the intention of the parties

D   Does not make any presumptions about the intention of the parties

22 The equitable remedy of rescission will

A   Order that the parties terminate their actions under the contract

B   Force the parties for any reasonable acts they have undertaken

C   Remunerate the parties for any reasonable acts they have undertaken

D   Order that the parties are places in their exact pre-contractual position

23 S offers to sell his car to B for £10,000 cash. At what point in time does the contract come into being?

A   When B accepts the offer

B   When B pays S the £10,000

C   When the agreement is written down

D   When the agreement is signed

24 D owes £4,000 to C. Two weeks before the debt is due for payment C approaches D and promises to accept £3,500 in full and final settlement if D will pay that sum immediately. D agrees and immediately pays £3,500 to C. Which of the following statements is/are correct?

(i)   C is bound by his promise as per common law

(ii)   C is estopped by equity from going back on his promise

A   (i) only

B   (ii) only

C   Both (i) and (ii)

D   Neither (i) nor (ii)

25 **A plc has been induced to enter into a contract by the fraudulent misrepresentation of B. Which of the following is *incorrect*?**

A   A plc may be able to rescind the contract

B   A plc may be able to claim damages and then rescind the contract

C   A plc is entitled either to rescind the contract or to claim the damages

D   A plc is entitled to refuse to perform the contract if it is still executory

26 **In the event of a breach of contract, the difference between a condition and a warranty is important because it determines**

A   The measure of damages available to the innocent party

B   The type of damages available to the innocent party

C   The remedy available to the innocent party

D   Whether or not the court will exercise its discretion to grant specific performance

27 **Builder Ltd increase the contracted price to erect an office block for Mega plc; the building is to be ready for occupation by the end of 2010. Due to Builder Ltd's lack of adherence to safety requirements, the Health and Safety Executive have issued a notice prohibiting further work on the site until safety measures as per its improvement notice are implemented by Builder Ltd.**

Which one of the following gives the correct position?

A   Builder Ltd increase the contract price to cover the costs of implementing the safety measures

B   Builder Ltd will be in breach of contract if it fails to complete the office block by the due date

C   If Builder Ltd fail to complete the office block by the due date it will not be in breach of contract, provided it shows that it has taken all reasonable steps to do so

D   The contract between Builder Ltd and Mega plc is frustrated by the HSE's actions

28 **Which of the following statements relating to remedies for breach of contract is/are correct?**

(i)   Damages will not be ordered where the claimant has acted unfairly.

(ii) Damages will not be ordered where specific performance is an adequate remedy.

A   (i) only

B   (ii) only

C   Both (i) and (ii)

D   Neither (i) nor (ii)

29 Steve, by letter, offered to sell Mack 800 tonnes of iron at £40 per ton "open till Tuesday". On Monday, Mack sent a telex to Steve inquiring if Steve "would accept £40 for delivery over two months". No reply was received, so later that day Mack sent a letter accepting the offer of £40 per ton which was posted first class and arrived on Tuesday. Meanwhile Steve had sold the goods to Dave on Monday evening and informed Mack by letter posted on that day. Mack sues Steve for breach of contract. What is his position?

    A   Mack will succeed. His telex was a mere inquiry and he had accepted Steve's offer by post and therefore the offer had not expired

    B   Mack will not succeed, his telex was a counteroffer which causes Steve's offer to lapse

    C   Mack will succeed, provided he can show that there was consideration for keeping the offer until Tuesday

    D   Mack will not succeed. The offer was revoked by Steve by letter on Monday before Mack's acceptance was received on the Tuesday

30 Robert's wife Kate, expressed the wish that Robert, if he survived her, should have the use of her house. After Kate's death her executor agreed to allow Robert to occupy the house (i) because of Kate's wishes and (ii) on the payment by Robert of £24 per year.

    Robert seeks to enforce this agreement and the executor wishes to avoid it in order to sell the house. What is the legal position?

    A   Robert can enforce the agreement on the basis of his deceased wife's wishes

    B   Robert cannot enforce the agreement because the promise to pay is not consideration

    C   Robert can enforce the agreement because the promise of £24 per year provides consideration for it

    D   Robert cannot enforce the agreement because £24 per year is not sufficient consideration

31 Frustration discharges a contract when

    A   A contract is impossible to perform at the time it is made

    B   An event occurs after the contract has been made rendering the performance more difficult and expensive to perform

    C   An event occurs after the contract has been made rendering its performance impossible

    D   A party expressly promises to do something which he later decided is not in his best interests

32 By deed, Victoria contracted to buy a herd of cows from Albert. She has failed to pay for them. Within what period of time must Albert bring an action to recover the amount owed to him?

    A   A reasonable period of time

    B   Six years

    C   Twelve years

    D   No limit

33 Which of the following contracts must be effected in the form of a deed to be enforceable?

A   A hire purchase contract

B   An agreement to guarantee the debt of another person

C   A contract to lend money

D   A promise in return for no consideration

34 A offers to sell certain goods to B for £150. B responds by sending a cheque to A for £140 and giving instructions for delivery of the goods. What is the effect of B's response?

A   It constitutes an acceptance of A's offer

B   It causes A's offer to lapse

C   It frustrates A's offer

D   It constitutes a counteroffer, thereby destroying A's offer

35 Rosemary offered by letter to sell Mary her motorbike for £5,000. Mary wrote back saying she accepted the offer and would pay in two instalments at the end of the two following months. Is there a contract?

A   No, because Mary is trying to amend the contractual terms, Rosemary can be assumed to revoke the offer

B   Yes, there has been an offer and acceptance and a binding contract applies

C   No, Mary's response constitutes a counteroffer and is effectively a rejection of Rosemary's offer

D   Yes, Mary's response is merely a clarification of contractual terms

36 Which of the following rules regarding consideration is *incorrect*?

A   Every simple contract must be supported by consideration

B   Consideration must move from the promisee

C   Consideration must be adequate

D   Consideration must be sufficient

37 A number of children, by their father's will, were entitled to a house after their mother's death. During the mother's life, one of the children and his wife lived with her in the house. The wife made various improvements to the house, and at a later date all the children signed a document addressed to her, stating that "in consideration of your carrying out certain alterations and improvements to the property, we hereby agree that the executors shall repay to you from the estate, when distributed, the sum of £488 in settlement of the amount spent on such improvements". The agreed sum was not paid. The wife's action to recover the sum will fail on the ground that

A   There was no intention to create legal relations

B   Past consideration is not consideration

C   The document should have been registered

D   The contract was illegal

38 **The doctrine of privity of contract means**

A   A contract is not legally binding if it is a private agreement

B   Only the parties to a contract can enforce it

C   The terms of a contract are primarily the concern of the parties to it

D   An ambiguity in the contract will be interpreted against the party trying to avoid liability

39 **Karen wrote to Joe and offered to sell her Ford Capri to him for £2,000. Joe wrote back saying that he accepted but would not be able to pay until the end of the month. Karen did not reply so Joe went to her office with £2,000 in cash and demanded the car. Is there a contract between Karen and Joe?**

A   Yes, as Karen has made a valid offer which Joe has accepted

B   Yes, as Joe's response was a request for further information and his action in bringing the money to Karen's office constitutes valid acceptance

C   No, as Joe's response constitutes a counteroffer which has the effect of destroying Karen's original offer

D   Yes, as Karen's initial offer stays open until expressly revoked

40 **Under the Sale of Goods Act 1979 (as amended), when is there an implied condition of satisfactory quality?**

A   Only if the seller is selling in the ordinary course of business

B   If the seller is selling in the course of business

C   If the seller is selling in the course of a business to a person buying as a consumer

D   In all contracts for the sale of goods

41 **An agreement to carry out an act already required by law amounts to**

A   Inadequate consideration

B   Illegal consideration

C   Past consideration

D   Insufficient consideration

THE LAW OF EMPLOYMENT

42 **Anne works for E plc under a 4-year fixed-term contract of employment. At the end of the 4 years, E plc fails to renew the contract because Anne is pregnant.**

Which of the following statements is /are correct?

(i)   Anne will succeed in an action against E plc for wrongful dismissal,

(ii)   Anne will succeed in an action against E plc for unfair dismissal.

A   (i) only

B   (ii) only

C   Both (i) and (ii)

D   Neither (i) nor (ii)

43 **Which of the following statements is /are correct?**

(i) An employer has an implied duty to behave reasonably and responsibly towards employees,

(ii) An employer has an implied duty to provide a reference.

A (i) only

B (ii) only

C Both (i) and (ii)

D Neither (i) nor (ii)

44 **An employee is entitled to the particulars of his employment:**

A Immediately on commencing employment

B After one month

C After two months

D After completing his trial period

45 **Which one of the following statements is *incorrect*?**

A It is automatically unfair to dismiss an employee for trade union activity

B It is automatically unfair to dismiss an employee who refuses to obey a reasonable instruction

C It is automatically unfair to dismiss an employee who becomes pregnant

D It is automatically unfair to dismiss an employee who complains on health and safety

46 **Which of the following statements is incorrect about wrongful dismissal?**

A It is a breach of contract

B It can be heard in both civil courts and employment tribunals

C It is a statutory right

D Liability is limited to the net pay for the maximum contractual-statutory notice period

47 **Which ONE of the following is an area of discrimination that is not prohibited by an Act of Parliament?**

A Disability

B Race

C Age

D Sex

48   Which ONE of the following is not accurate in relation to the duties owed to employees by employers.

   A   There is a duty to combine staff and equipment into a reasonably safe system of working

   B   The duty of care in providing equipment is satisfied by purchasing the equipment from a reputable supplier.

   C   A duty exists to give proper instruction and training in the use of equipment

   D   A duty exists to dismiss any employee whose behaviour is dangerous

49   How many Regulations have resulted from the directives introduced relating to controls imposed on employers related to health and safety?

   A   4

   B   5

   C   6

   D   8

COMPANY ADMINISTRATION

50   The directors of a company are considering altering the company's Articles of Association. The alteration must be *bona fide* for the benefit of

   A   Members and creditors

   B   All current and future members

   C   The company as a whole

   D   The majority of the membership

51   What is the quorum for a general meeting of a registered company?

   A   Two persons being members of proxies for members

   B   Three persons being members of proxies for members

   C   Two persons being members

   D   Three persons being members

52   Which of the following statements is/are *correct*?

   (i)   The partners in an ordinary partnership jointly own the firm's assets

   (ii)   The shareholders in a company jointly own the company's assets

   A   (i) only

   B   (ii) only

   C   Both (i) and (ii)

   D   Neither (i) nor (ii)

53   The Articles of Association of ABC Ltd provide that all disputes between ABC Ltd and its directors must be referred to arbitration. Del is a director of ABC Ltd and is in dispute with the company about late payment of his director's fees.

Which of the following is/are *correct*?

(i)   Del is obliged by the Articles of Association to refer the dispute to arbitration whether or not he is a shareholder.

(ii)   Del is obliged by the Articles of Association to refer the dispute to arbitration only if he is a shareholder.

A   (i) only

B   (ii) only

C   Both (i) and (ii)

D   Neither (i) nor (ii)

54   To what extent is a member of a company limited by guarantee personally liable for the company's debts.

A   He is personally liable for all the company's debts at any time

B   He is personally liable for all the company's debts on a winding up

C   His personal liability is limited to the amount identified in the statement of guarantee upon a winding up

D   His personal liability is limited to the amount stated in the statement of guarantee at any time

55   Under the Companies Act 2006, what is the consequence of the number of members of a public company falling below two?

A   The company must cease trading within six months

B   The remaining member becomes jointly and severally liable with the company for the company's debts after six months

C   The company must notify the Registrar, but otherwise can continue trading as normal

D   The remaining member automatically takes over personal liability for the company's debts incurred while he is the sole member

56   Which of the following is a requirement for any public company registered in England?

A   No restriction may be placed on the transfer of its shares

B   Its shares must be publicly for sale

C   It must have a minimum paid up capital of £50,000

D   The final words of the company's name must be 'Public Limited Company' or PLC

57 Immediately prior to the incorporation of Products Ltd, Roberts, one of its promoters, bought property in his own name from Suppliers Ltd. He later sold the property to Products Ltd at a large profit without disclosure.

To whom is Roberts liable in relation to this secret profit?

A   Suppliers Ltd

B   Products Ltd

C   The promoters of Products Ltd

D   The shareholders of Products Ltd

58 Which of the following names could not without further consent be a permissible name under the Companies Act for a company, the main object of which is to contract refuse collection services for Westchester City Council?

A   Westchester City Refuse Services Ltd

B   Council (Refuse Collection) Services Ltd

C   Refuse Collection (Westchester) Ltd

D   City Waste Disposal Ltd

59 The Memorandum of Association of a company must be signed by

A   The subscribers and all the directors

B   The subscribers and at least one of the directors

C   The subscribers and the company secretary

D   The subscribers only

60 Ceres plc last held an AGM on 31 October 2007. When must the company hold its next AGM?

A   31 October 2009

B   31 December 2009

C   Within 6 month period after the accounting reference date

D   Within 3 month period after the accounting reference date

61 For which of the following is an ordinary resolution of the shareholders sufficient authority?

A   To amend a private company's articles

B   To alter a public company's objects

C   To change a private company's name

D   To give directors authority to issue new shares

62 **The clause in the memorandum of association of an existing company limited by shares sets out the amount of:**

A   Total authorised capital

B   Authorised capital divided into shares of fixed amount

C   Authorised capital divided into classes of shares of a fixed amount

D   The issued capital in shares of fixed amount

63 **What is the liability of a member of an unlimited company?**

A   To pay a call without limit on a winding up

B   For the debts while he is a member

C   For the debts on a winding up

D   To pay a call to pay the debts at any time

64 **Popeye is the promoter of Spinach Ltd. He and his wife Olive are the first directors of the company. Popeye sold a plot of land he owned to the company making a profit of £20,000. What is the legal position regarding the profit?**

A   Popeye may keep the profit in any event

B   Popeye may keep the profit as long as it is disclosed to the board of directors

C   Popeye may keep the profit as long as it is disclosed to the first shareholders of the company

D   Popeye may not keep the profit under any circumstances

65 **Dave and Sue have applied to have Bideford Ltd registered as a private company limited by shares but failed to submit articles of association to the Registrar. What is the effect of the omission to the Registrar?**

A   The Registrar will return the application to Dave and Sue

B   A provisional registration will be made but Bideford will be unable to commence trading until the submission of its articles

C   Provisional registration will be permitted pending determination of the articles at the first meeting of the directors

D   Model form articles will automatically apply to the company

66 **What proportion of a company's shareholders may object to a special resolution passed to change the company's name under the terms of the Companies Act 2006?**

A   15 per cent of any class of shareholder

B   15 per cent of the shareholders

C   10 per cent of any class of shareholder

D   There is no statutory right of objection

67 Shorter notice than that required for an AGM of a plc is permitted with a minimum member support of:

    A   75%

    B   80%

    C   90%

    D   95%

68 Under s40 Companies Act 2006, what is the position of a person innocently entering into an *ultra vires* contract with a company and decided on by the directors of that company?

    A   The contract is void and no action may be taken on it

    B   The validity of the contract cannot be challenged on the ground of lack of capacity

    C   The third party can only sue the directors in person for exceeding their powers

    D   The contract is unenforceable but the third party can retain any property received under it

69 Shareholders in a private company can pass a written ordinary resolution with support of

    A   100%

    B   95%

    C   80%

    D   50%+

70 Shareholders in a private company can pass a written special resolution with support of

    A   100%

    B   95%

    C   75%

    D   51%+

71 All companies can communicate electronically with shareholders so long as appropriate approval exists. What is the appropriate approval required?

    A   Approval of 100% members

    B   With member consent in general meeting only

    C   With a provision in the articles of association only

    D   With either consent in general meeting or provision in the articles of association

72 Where a member or debenture holder receives information from the company electronically, on request for a hard copy of the documentation which ONE of the following is correct? The company

    A   Must provide a hard copy of the relevant information at a nominal charge

    B   Must provide a hard copy of the relevant information at no charge

    C   Can refuse to provide a hard copy

    D   Must provide a hard copy to members free of charge but to debenture holders at a nominal charge

73 Which ONE of the following is NOT applicable to private companies under the Companies Act 2006?

A   No longer will it be necessary to hold Annual General Meetings

B   A written special resolution must be passed by the members representing a three-quarters majority of the total voting rights

C   Companies can communicate electronically with members as a matter of course

D   A written ordinary resolution can be passed with a simple majority vote of the total voting rights

COMPANY FINANCE AND MANAGEMENT

74 Gulliver Ltd has recently dismissed one of its directors. Gulliver Ltd wishes to pay Joe compensation for loss of office. Who must approve this payment?

A   The board of directors

B   The Inland Revenue

C   The creditors

D   The shareholders in a general meeting

75 Under the Companies Act 2006, a property transaction exceeding £100,000 in value made between the company and one of its directors and not approved by the company in general meeting is

A   Valid

B   Voidable at the instance of the company

C   Voidable at the instance of the director

D   Void

76 Toffee plc has authorised share capital of 50,000 £1 shares of which 25,000 are issued and quoted on the stock exchange at 80 pence per share. Toffee plc now wishes to issue the remaining 25,000. At which of the following prices could the shares be issued?

A   25 pence per share

B   80 pence per share

C   95 pence per share

D   £1 per share

77 Which one of the following statements is incorrect?

A   A director can be an employee of the company

B   A director can be an independent contractor of the company

C   A shareholder can be an employee of the company

D   A partner can be an employee of the firm

78   **A private company, limited by shares must be registered with**

    A   At least one member, who may also be the sole director and company secretary

    B   At least one member, who may also be the sole director or the company secretary

    C   At least one member, who cannot also act as a director or company secretary

    D   At least two members, one of whom may act as a director and the other as company secretary

79   **In relation to companies limited by shares, which one of the following statements regarding issue of shares is *correct*?**

    A   Shares may not be issued at a discount to the market value

    B   A public company cannot issue shares in return for work or services

    C   A private company may not allot a share unless it is paid up to at least a quarter on the nominal value

    D   Neither public nor private companies may issue shares for a non-cash consideration unless that consideration has been independently valued and reported on

80   **In relation to a floating charge, which one of the following is incorrect?**

    A   It can not be created over land

    B   It is charged over assets present and future

    C   The company may freely dispose of the charged assets in the ordinary course of its business

    D   The assets subject to the charge will change from time to time

81   **S172 Companies Act 2006 requires directors to have regard to the interests of the company employees. If directors fail to satisfy this requirement action may be taken against them by**

    (i)   the company

    (ii)   the employees

    Which of the above is/are correct?

    A   (i) only

    B   (ii) only

    C   Both (i) and (ii)

    D   Neither (i) nor (ii)

82 The liquidator of ABC Ltd has successfully brought proceedings against one of its directors for wrongful trading under s214 of the Insolvency Act 1986. The court may

(i) Order the director to make contributions to the company's assets.

(ii) Impose a fine on the director.

A (i) only

B (ii) only

C Both (i) and (ii)

D Neither (i) nor (ii)

83 S994 of the Companies Act 2006 allows a petition to be made to the court for relief from unfair prejudice. Which one of the following statements as to who may petition is correct?

A Any member

B Any director

C Any employee

D The company

84 A director who is in breach of his fiduciary duty to the company which does not involve a fraud on the minority may be exempted from liability by:

A A resolution passed by a general meeting

B A resolution passed by the board of directors

C A provision in the Memorandum of Association

D A provision in the Articles of Association

85 What type of resolution is required at a general meeting to remove a director from office?

A An ordinary resolution

B An ordinary resolution with special notice

C A special resolution

D A special resolution with special notice

86 Which of the following share issues would be deemed to be for the proper purpose?

A An issue to a potential bidder to facilitate his takeover bid for the company

B An issue to raise finance for a new building project

C An issue to a nominee in order to prevent a takeover bid

D An issue to a director to increase his voting power and so to allow him to ratify his actions

87   **A floating charge is a charge:**

   A   On a class of current assets which can be identified

   B   On the undertaking of a company

   C   On a class of assets which may change in the ordinary course of business

   D   On a class of assets, present or future, which may change in the ordinary course of business

88   **What is the position of a minority shareholder who wishes to bring an action in the company's name against the directors who are the majority shareholders and have purchased company assets at considerable undervaluation?**

   A   No action can be brought by the minority

   B   An action may only be brought if there is a deliberate fraud on the part of the directors

   C   An action will be allowed only if the Articles of Association permit

   D   An action will be permitted since the directors have used their position to make a personal gain at the expense of the company

89   **Larry, an entertainer, is a director and a majority shareholder of Lamb Ltd which has no significant assets. He has no contract of employment with Lamb Ltd. John contracts with Lamb Ltd for Larry to appear at a concert. Larry fails to appear and John loses a large sum of money. John has a legal remedy against**

   A   Lamb Ltd

   B   Larry, as a director of Lamb Ltd

   C   Larry, as the owner of Lamb Ltd

   D   Larry, on the basis that the company is a sham

90   **In relation to companies and charities formed after October 2009 which of the following is correct?**

   A   Companies and charities have no contractual restrictions on their contractual capacity.

   B   Companies cannot impose restrictions and limitations on their contractual activities.

   C   Company restrictions and limitations on commercial activities must be identified in the company articles of association.

   D   Company restrictions and limitations on contractual activities must be identified in the company memorandum of association.

91   **Which of the following is not a legitimate use of the share premium account?**

   A   Writing-off a discount on the issue of debentures

   B   Writing-off underwriting commission

   C   Writing-off preliminary expenses

   D   Writing-off a discount on the issue of shares

92 Orpheus has for many years, with the knowledge of the other directors, acted as managing director of Underworld Ltd. Although the Articles of Underworld Ltd empower the directors to appoint one of their member as managing director, they have never actually done so formally. Orpheus, in his capacity as managing director, entered a number of contracts with Hades plc. After a serious internal dispute between Orpheus and the other directors, Underworld is now refusing to honour the contract with Hades plc. What is the legal position?

A Underworld Ltd will not be bound by the contracts made by Orpheus as he has not been properly appointed as managing director of the company and therefore does not as such have contractual capacity

B Neither Orpheus personally nor Underworld Ltd will be bound by the contracts made by Orpheus as his lack of contractual capacity as managing director has effectively rendered the contracts void

C Underworld Ltd will be bound by the contracts made by Orpheus as he had apparent authority to make them, having been held out by the board as having the appropriate authority

D Underworld Ltd will be bound by the contracts made by Orpheus as he had actual authority to make them by virtue of his position as de facto managing director

93 Who will be liable for wrongful trading on an insolvent winding up?

A All persons who took part in it

B All persons who knew the company was insolvent

C Directors of the company

D Any officer of the company

94 What authority is required for a private company to provide financial assistance for the principle purpose of the purchase of its own shares?

A No authority is needed

B Special resolution and statutory declaration

C No authority is needed unless it is a subsidiary of a public company

D Special resolution, statutory declaration, auditors' report and court approval

95 Under s561 CA2006, there is a statutory right of pre-emption on allotment of shares by a company. This applies when:

A A shareholder wishes to sell his shares

B The company allots shares for cash

C The company allots equity shares for cash

D The company allots equity shares

96 What is the status of a loan of £20,000 made by Snippet plc, a manufacturing company, to a director to enable him to renovate her kitchen?

A Prohibited by the Companies Act 2006

B Prohibited unless made in the ordinary course of business

C Prohibited, unless made for improvements to her residence and available to employers

D Valid, provided sanctioned by ordinary resolution

97 How may a company (i) ratify an *ultra vires* contract entered into by directors and (ii) agree to relieve those directors from liability?

Is it

A (i) and (ii) by separate resolution

B (i) and (ii) by one special resolution

C (i) by special resolution and (ii) by ordinary resolution

D (i) cannot be rectified and (ii) by special resolution

98 In what circumstances may a company director incur personal liability for the debts of a company?

Is it on

A Wrongful trading

B Fraudulent trading

C Winding up

D Acting as a director contrary to a disqualification order

99 In which ONE of the following areas will the CA2006 not apply to both public and private companies?

A Memorandum of Association

B Articles of Association

C Company Secretary

D Board meetings

100 Under the CA1985 directors were required to have information of their home address on file at Companies House. The CA2006 introduces a change to this requirement. Which ONE of the following will be applicable?

A A director's home address and service address must be on public record

B A service address only need be on public record

C The company address will be deemed appropriate

D No address for a director will be on record or be required

ETHICS AND BUSINESS

101 **Which of these is the most accurate statement of when an accountant should act, having identified a threat to ethical conduct:**

    A   when there is a substantial threat to the profession or their firm?

    B   when there is a possibility of some professional liability?

    C   when there is anything other than an insignificant consequence?

102 **Ethical frameworks can draw both on rules and on framework principles. Which of the following best expresses the complementary role of ethical rules and principles?**

    A   Ethical rules outline the things you must do and the way you should do them, while framework principles provide guidance on things you ought to do, but leave you to determine how to comply

    B   Ethical rules provide for conduct that must be complied with in a particular way, while framework principles provide the reasons why standards and rules must be complied with

    C   Ethical rules provide a clear means to identify what you must do, while framework principles provide the means to identify, evaluate and address ethical problems

103 **Which of the following statements are true?**

    A   An accountant is under no duty to disclose the limitations of their expertise to the client

    B   An accountant is only responsible for his or her own professional qualifications and training

    C   An accountant may need to compromise the most precise attention to detail in preparing work in order to meet a reasonable deadline

104 **Consider the list of safeguards for ethical conduct and choose which are primary workplace (internal) safeguards (A) and which are regulatory (external) safeguards (B).**

Try to match internal safeguards to their external counterparts.

    1   Appropriate disciplinary processes

    2   Code of Ethics

    3   Continuing professional development requirements

    4   Corporate governance regulations

    5   Educational, training and experience requirements for entry into the profession

    6   Effective, well-publicised complaints systems operated by the employing organisation, the profession or a regulator, which enable colleagues, employers and members of the public to draw attention to unprofessional or unethical behaviour

    7   External review by a legally empowered third party of the reports, returns, communications or information produced by a professional accountant

    8   Leadership that stresses the importance of ethical behaviour and the expectation that employees will act in an ethical manner

9   Policies and procedures to implement and monitor the quality of employee performance

10   Professional or regulatory monitoring and disciplinary procedures

11   Professional standards

12   Recruitment procedures in the employing organisation emphasising the importance of employing high calibre competent staff

13   Strong internal controls

14   The employing organisation's ethics and conduct programmes

15   The employing organisation's systems of corporate oversight or other oversight structures

16   Timely communication of the employing organisation's policies and procedures, including any changes to them, to all employees and appropriate training and education on such policies and procedures

17   Policies and procedures to empower and encourage employees to communicate to senior levels within the employing organisation any ethical issues that concern them without fear of retribution

18   An explicitly stated duty to report breaches of ethical requirements

105   Which of these are ethical reasons for the need for continuous improvement and lifelong learning?

A   Because they are essential for career progression

B   Because qualifications are important so the public can see that accountants are capable

C   Because the world of accountancy is constantly developing and it is the accountant's duty to keep up

D   Because otherwise there may be costly mistakes made

E   Because learning is a good thing in itself

F   Because firms are audited for the qualifications of their staff

106   Which of these are *explicitly* virtues promoted by the CIMA Code of practice?

A   Reliability

B   Accuracy

C   Diversity awareness

D   Financial responsibility

E   Social responsibility

F   Loyalty

G   Courtesy

H   Fidelity

I   Punctuality

J   Respect

107 **Does an accountant breach his duty of integrity if the accountant:**

A   Leaves a client to discover important information that is freely available?

B   Only tells the client the information they have specifically asked for or that is habitually provided?

C   Forgets to mention something important?

D   Withholds information that may be compromising for the employer?

108 **Which of the following is true?**

A   It is acceptable to discuss client information with a person who knows nothing about your job or business

B   Prospective or past clients are owed a lesser duty of confidentiality than current clients

C   Nothing learned as a consequence of working for one client may be used in relation to another

109 **Identify the statement that best describes the relationship between CIMA's Code of Ethics and that of IFAC:**

A   The CIMA Code is a framework, whereas IFAC provides the rules

B   The IFAC Code is a framework, whereas the CIMA Code provides the rules

C   Both are essentially the same frameworks, but CIMA's Code has been adjusted to meet local regulatory conditions

D   The IFAC Code is an important guidance, but you can get disciplined for breaching CIMA's Code

110 **Which of the following statements is true?**

A   The Financial Reporting Council is a government body which regulates the ethics for the profession

B   The Professional Oversight Body for Accountancy decides on what changes need to be made to the professional rules and puts new ethical rules into place

C   The Auditing Practices Board advises, consults on and sets Ethical Standards for auditors

111 **Which of these is not a Principle of Standards in Public Life?**

A   Transparency

B   Honesty

C   Accountability

112 **Corporate responsibility means**

A   That the company, not the individual is ultimately responsible for the values of the accounting professionals it employs

B   That a company has the responsibility to do what is in the best interests of its clients, employees and shareholders

C   That a company has to ensure that it has a charitable and environmentally friendly marketing approach

D   That a company reviews and considers the impact of its policies and practices to ensure that plays a positive and contributory role in relation to its stakeholders, the community and the environment

113 **What three Rs, together with Timeliness and Courtesy, constitute the Personal Qualities one would expect of a Professional Accountant?**

A   Regulation, Registration, Remuneration

B   Respect, Reliability, Realism

C   Reliability, Responsibility, Regulation

D   Respect, Responsibility, Reliability

114 **When might it be appropriate for an accountant to disclose information, provided in confidence?**

A   At the request of the client

B   At the request of the regulator

C   At the request of a solicitor

D   At the request of the employer

115 **In respect of the following problem situations, would you refer primarily to (A) the IFAC Code, (B) the CIMA Code, (C) the Law, or (D) apply professional judgement:**

1   A request to disclose data relating to a client to a non-accounting regulatory body, for example the Inland Revenue

2   A dispute over the proper returns relating to an off-shore company and whether you have an ethical duty to apply a higher level of compliance than is required by the foreign jurisdiction's law

3   Pressure being exerted as a result of a change of government policy on the public sector client you are working for

4   Disclosing information you have in your possession, that has not been actually requested, but might assist an investigation by CIMA into alleged ethical wrongdoing

ETHICAL CONFLICT

116   Classify the following (A) to (B), according to the situations below (1-5):

A   Self-interest threats

B   Self-review threats

C   Advocacy threats

D   Familiarity threats

E   Intimidation threats

1   Preparing accounts for a campaign group of which the accountant is a leading member

2   Preparing accounts under an unrealistically imposed deadline by a major client

3   Preparing accounts for your close relative's business

4   Preparing accounts for your spouse's business

5   Preparing accounts and providing a basic audit function on those accounts

117   Which of the following statements are true?

A   An accountant will not be in breach of the CIMA Code of Ethics where the accountant has inadvertently compromised an ethical principle, so long as he remedies his mistake as soon as possible, following the appropriate safeguards

B   An accountant is not obliged to evaluate threats that might compromise ethical principles if he has no actual knowledge of the problem

C   An accountant should consider non-financial circumstances known about a situation, as well as the financial data presented when considering a threat to ethical standards

D   An accountant should refuse to work for a client or resign his job if he is unable to apply appropriate ethical safeguards

118   Which of these correctly outlines the process for addressing ethical problems?

A   Identify the potential for ethical conflict and avoid it, otherwise seeks guidance from CIMA, a manager or a legal adviser

B   Identify the facts, apply the framework, seek an internal resolution, ask CIMA

C   Identify any principles involved, follow internal procedures, apply the Code if that does not resolve it and then ask CIMA

D   Identify the facts, the issues of ethics, principles of the Code involved, use the internal procedures and if all else fails, ask CIMA

119   Where there is no safeguard provided by professional standards, but an accountant has encountered a threat, should the accountant:

    A   weigh up the likelihood of harm and cautiously applying good sense? or

    B   take legal advice before proceeding? or

    C   avoid the activity altogether?

120   Where an accountant encounters a fraud the disclosure of which would be a breach of professional confidence, should the accountant:

    A   maintain their duty of confidence?

    B   disclose the fraud immediately?

    C   take legal advice or consult CIMA?

121   Under which of these circumstances might it be permissible to disclose client information:

    A   when the client has asked you to disclose and you are lawfully entitled to do so?

    B   to help a colleague defend a professional misconduct claim?

    C   to assist in undertaking a review or audit for professional standards purposes?

    D   to help provide an accurate budgetary statement for the employer?

    E   to respond to a solicitor's letter, representing someone suing the client?

Case study

You are approached by your colleague Sima, who has received a complaint from a client (1) because she has not been able to produce a promised report on time (2). Sima says that this is because there is a new software system that she has not got to grips with yet (3), because she could not make it to the training event (4). Sima would like you to contact the client to tell them that there has been a problem with the system (5). She tells you more than you wish to know (6) about the background to the client's request. Office practice is for this type of report to be checked by a colleague before being sent out. Sima says that she has checked her own report, but asks you to sign it off without looking at it (7). You and Sima are friends and so you want to help (8). She says there is a drink in it for you (9) if you help. She also tells you not to tell anyone in case she gets into trouble (10).

122   Which of the actions in the case study compromise integrity?

123   Which of the actions in the case study compromise objectivity?

124   Which of the actions in the case study compromise professional competence and due care?

125   Which of the actions in the case study compromise confidentiality?

126   Which of the actions in the case study compromise professional behaviour?

127   Your boss approaches you to attend a reception on her behalf to represent the firm to the client. You deal with a competitor firm as your own client. There is nothing you are aware of that makes you think that either firm would have a problem with it, but it makes you a little uneasy. Would you:

A   Ignore the problem and do as your boss asks;

B   Decline on the basis that you have a (fictional) alternative engagement;

C   Accept and not tell the other client on the basis that what they do not know will not hurt them;

D   Consider the facts and the likelihood of a conflict of interests somewhere down the line and go if you can see no likely difficulty;

E   Ask the other client whether they mind you going?

128   You have failed to make a record of a piece of work on a client's account. It would mean that you would not be able to bill the client for it under the firm's billing procedure. You are pretty sure that you remember sufficient details to put in a realistic guesstimate. Do you:

A   enter the guesstimate and get on with another job?

B   leave the entry blank, so the firm cannot claim for your time?

C   contact the client and explain the situation at the risk of undermining their confidence in the firm?

D   tell the boss and wait for the explosion?

129   Which of the following would be of use when trying to find a resolution to a serious ethical breach?

A   CIMA

B   Board of your Organisation

C   Audit Committee of your Organisation

D   Legal and Compliance Department

E   Your solicitors

F   Your line-manager

130   What is the most important first step when dealing with a potential ethical problem?

A   Tell your boss

B   Read the CIMA Code of Practice

C   Make a thorough and rapid check of the facts

D   Ask a colleague their opinion

CORPORATE GOVERNANCE

131 Corporate governance is not concerned with which one of the following?

A   Effective control

B   Business efficacy

C   Fiduciary duties

D   Accountability

132 Fiduciary duties were created by which one of the following?

A   The European Union

B   The Common Law

C   The Courts of Equity

D   The Combined Code

133 In the scandal involving Enron information relating to which one of the following was withheld in order to maintain confidence in its stocks?

A   Corporate losses

B   Corporate borrowing

C   Director remuneration

D   Company reorganisation

134 Within the European Union, developments have taken place in the area of corporate governance, but how have these developments been introduced?

A   With the issue of directives

B   With a code of corporate governance

C   With a regulation effective in all member states

D   With the creation of a governance and auditing practice code

135 The European Union established an EU Corporate Governance Forum to coordinate corporate governance developments in member states. How many members does the forum have?

A   12

B   15

C   18

D   25

136 In which one of the following committees' reports was it recommended that executive directors should have service contracts of no longer than three years?

A   The Cadbury Committee Report

B   The Greenbury Committee Report

C   The Hampel Committee Report

D   The Higgs Committee Report

Section 3

ANSWERS TO PRACTICE QUESTIONS

COMPARISON OF ENGLISH LAW WITH ALTERNATIVE LEGAL SYSTEMS

1

    (a)   Orders in Council are a form of *delegated legislation* enacted by the *Privy Council*. Individual ministers can create ministerial regulations that are also known as *statutory instruments*.

    (b)   Parking regulations are introduced by *local authorities* in the form of bye-laws. Advantages of this form of law making include speed and *flexibility*.

2

    (a)   Within the European Union a *codified* system of law is found in a significant number of states. European Community Law became part of the United Kingdom law as a result of the *European Communities Act*.

    (b)   In the European Union the Council of Ministers makes decisions only by *unanimous decision*. It is the Commission that makes *Regulations*.

THE LAW OF CONTRACT

3

    (a)   In Contract Law an offer can be made to the *world at large*.

    (b)   To be effective an acceptance to an offer must be *absolute* and *unqualified*.

    (c)   Both parties to a contract must provide consideration, and the consideration must be *sufficient;* however, the consideration need not be *adequate*.

4

    (a)   Promissory estoppel can only be used as a *shield* and not a *sword*.

    (b)   The doctrine of promissory estoppel is based on the principles of *equity* and its effect is only *suspensory*.

5

    (a)   Where a breach of condition occurs, the innocent party can repudiate the contract and sue for damages. If the innocent party affirms the contract on such a breach, he can sue for damages.

    (b)   Contract terms can be implied at common law where there is a lack of *business efficacy*. Terms are implied under the Sale of Goods Act 1979, which primarily seek to protect the consumer.

    (c)   Without this statutory protection the rule of *caveat emptor* which means l*et the buyer beware* would apply.

6

    (a)   Silence cannot constitute misrepresentation. However, certain exceptions to this rule exist. These include where a change *in circumstances* is found. Also where a contract *uberrimae fidei* is found. This Latin term means of the *utmost good faith.*

    (b)   Three types of misrepresentation are recognised: innocent, negligent and *fraudulent.* The equitable remedy of *rescission* which serves to restore the parties to their pre-contract position may be available.

THE LAW OF EMPLOYMENT

7

    (a)   When considering the question of whether or not a person is an employee or an independent contractor, the economic reality test can be used in arriving at a decision. Factors relevant when applying this test include regularity of *payment methods*, and *obligations* and *hours*. A further test that is relevant is the Integration test. This is sometimes also referred to as the *organisation test*.

    (b)   Whilst an employee has a contract *of service*, an independent contractor has a contract *for services*.

8

    (a)   Employers can be *vicariously* liable for the *torts* of employees.

    (b)   The Equal Pay Act 1970 prohibits pay differentials between male and female workers. An exception exists, however, where the employer can show a *genuine material difference*.

COMPANY ADMINISTRATION

9

(a)　There are two kinds of corporation, the corporation *sole* and the corporation *aggregate.*

(b)　The registered company is one kind of corporation *aggregate.* The registered company is an artificial *legal person.*

(c)　A veil of incorporation is recognised when a company is registered. However, the veil will be lifted under Sec. 213 of the Insolvency Act 1986 due to any *fraudulent* trading being found and Sec. 214 Insolvency Act 1986 where *wrongful* trading is found.

10

(a)　Under the Companies Act 2006 it is the *articles* of association that sets out the company's constitution. Public and private companies must have a certificate of incorporation. In addition, a public company must have a *trading certificate* before it can commence commercial activity.

(b)　A private company can be re-registered as a public company on the passing of a *special* resolution. Equally, a public company can be reregistered as a private company. An objection can be brought by a minimum 50 members or the holders of at least *5%* holders of issued shares.

COMPANY FINANCE AND MANAGEMENT

11

(a)　Anyone under the age of *16* cannot act as a director of a company. Directors must retire by rotation every third year. A director can be removed on the passing of an ordinary resolution. However, special notice of the resolution must be given.

(b)　A director owes fiduciary duties to his company which involves the use of powers for a *proper purpose* and also the avoidance of a *conflict of interest.*

12

(a)　The process by which a floating charge becomes a fixed charge is known as *crystallisation.* Debentures are usually secured by a *charge.*

(b)　Charges must be registered with the Registrar of Companies within *21* days. The debenture holder is a *creditor* of the company.

(c)　A company can deal with its property in the ordinary course of business even though that property is subject to a charge so long as it is a *floating* charge. Capital maintenance rules *do not* apply to debenture holders.

13

(a)   Private companies can provide financial assistance for the acquisition of their shares. The provision of financial assistance by a public company is a *criminal offence*.

(b)   Companies are not permitted to acquire their own shares; however, acquisition will occur after the issuing of *redeemable shares*. Further, in consequence of a *court order*, a company acquisition of its shares must take place.

14

(a)   Any member of a company can bring an action under Sec. 994 Companies Act 2006 on the basis of *unfairly prejudicial conduct*. An individual member can also bring a *representative* action to enforce a personal entitlement. At common law, actions could be brought under an exception to the rule in the case of *Foss v Harbottle*.

(b)   A minority of members of at least *10%* can require directors to convene a General Meeting, whilst a minimum *5%* members can demand a resolution be added at an Annual General Meeting.

(c)   A private company need not comply with the requirement for the annual appointment of *auditors*. Shorter notice than the required 14 days for a General meeting of a private company will be valid where a minimum *90%* of the members with voting rights agree.

CORPORATE GOVERNANCE

15

(a)   The Cadbury Committee defined corporate governance as "the system by which companies are *directed and controlled*".

(b)   Under the Combined Code a *disclosure* obligation exists with compliance with the Code being *voluntary*.

16

(a)   The unitary board structure in the UK is classified into three groups that are 1. *the all executive board*, 2. *the majority executive board* and 3. *the majority non-executive board*.

(b)   In France, the board and structure includes a two-tier board made up of 1. *the supervisory board* and 2. *the management committee*. The unitary board in France is recognised with combined and separate functions of the *chairman and chief executive*.

Section 4

ANSWERS TO OBJECTIVE TEST QUESTIONS

COMPARISON OF ENGLISH LAW WITH ALTERNATIVE LEGAL SYSTEMS

1   A

The duty of care applicable to John will be the same as that applied to any other vehicle driver. Different degrees or levels of negligence are not recognised. The duty of care is determined on the same basis irrespective of differing factors, for example here the level of inexperience and skill as a driver of John.

2   A

It is the type of injury that must be reasonably foreseeable. The extent of the injury may well be relevant in determining the size of damages awarded but is not relevant in determining the issue of liability. Equally the nature of the injury is irrelevant, so long as injury can be established.

3   D

Where the plaintiff relies on *Res Ip so Loquitur* they are in effect acknowledging that it is not necessary to prove breach of duty by the defendant. If breach of duty is established and damage can be identified, the view of the plaintiff may be that breach of the duty must have occurred. In this situation the burden of proof shifts to the defendant, and they can look to establishing that there was no breach. Important in this regard is the fact that the standard of proof in civil actions is on a balance of probabilities only.

4   C

It is necessary to establish that a duty of care was owed, that a breach of that duty occurred and that damage resulted. It is not appropriate to deal with intention. This is relevant with criminal actions. For this tort it is important to establish the issue of human error, mistake or inadvertence which separates the base for a civil action claim from a criminal action.

5   C

Vicarious liability applies where an employee commits a civil wrong whilst acting in the course of their employment. Vicarious liability will not apply where an employee has committed a crime, or where the relevant conduct is outside the requirements of the terms of employment, in other words they act 'on a frolic of their own'. The company will therefore only be liable for the conduct of Edward.

6   B

The law recognises a differing burden attaching to occupiers in relation to warnings of dangers given. What is an adequate warning to adults may not be seen as adequate to children. A greater responsibility is owed to children. A warning can be sufficient and enable the occupier to avoid liability.

7   B

The damages payable will be determined on the basis of the actual loss suffered by the innocent party. The level of loss can vary and so the size of damages can differ, subject to the differing level of loss. You take your victim as you find them.

8   D

The procedure to be followed in order that a Parliamentary Bill can become an Act of Parliament includes a third reading and a committee stage. When the Bill is ultimately passed by both Houses of Parliament it does not then automatically become an Act of Parliament. It is only when Royal Assent is received that the Bill becomes an Act.

9   D

The standard of proof to be satisfied in civil actions, not criminal actions, is on a balance of probabilities. In criminal actions, the case must be proved beyond reasonable doubt. The words 'every' and 'any' are inappropriate for use.

10   C

A decision is binding on only those parties to whom it is directed. Further, a directive is not directly applicable, it must be introduced through legislation of the member state in order to become law. An enactment is an Act of Parliament, so inappropriate. It is the regulation that automatically becomes law in member states. Treaties also apply automatically.

11   A

Whereas in England, Parliament has law-making powers, in the European Union it is the Council of Ministers rather than the Parliament that fulfils this function. The European Commission as an institution of the European Union plays a part in the process but is not a law maker, and the European Court of Justice has a primary role related to interpretation of law and addressing disputes.

12   D

The courts can look to the question of whether or not a minister on introducing statutory instruments has acted beyond his power or *ultra vires*. It is on this basis that the courts can exert control. Other factors identified do not truly stand as a basis for positive judicial control.

13   D

An *obiter dicta* statement is a statement made 'by the way' or 'in passing'. It will be additional to the *ratio decidendi*. A 'by the way' statement is not binding on any court. However, where the statement is made by the House of Lords* or Court of Appeal it can be particularly influential, but it does not have to be followed.

14   C

Orders in Council are made by the Privy Council and the Crown as delegated legislation. Statutory instruments are another form of delegated legislation usually made by government ministers. Bye-laws are introduced as delegated legislation by local authorities and public bodies. It is judicial precedent that is not delegated legislation. Precedent arises out of the decisions of the courts.

15   A

Statute prevails over decisions of the courts, even the House of Lords*. The House of Lords* is the highest domestic court. No right of appeal exists on domestic matters to the European Court of Justice. The House of Lords* is not bound by its previous decisions following the Practice Statement of 1966. The House can depart from its previous decisions where it is believed that is the right thing to do.

16   D

It is the 'literal rule' that requires the ordinary meaning of words to be applied where only one meaning is possible. If a word has more than one meaning then the court can apply the meaning that avoids an absurd result. This is the 'golden rule'.

17   C

English Law was influential in the development of the law in Hong Kong and Macau. However, Portuguese law was also influential in the development of law and a legal system in both countries.

*now Supreme Court

THE LAW OF CONTRACT

18   C

Generally advertisements are invitations to treat and not offers. It is the party who responds to the advert who can provide the offer which is then accepted or rejected. The *Carlill v Carbolic Smokeball Co.* case provides an exception to the norm. In this case the court held the advert constituted an offer to the world at large.

19   A

If a contract is void it is unenforceable by either contracting party. No rights at law can attach to the parties at law in relation to the contract. Repudiation is not necessary, equally the issue relating to further performance is irrelevant.

20   C

When an acceptance is communicated by fax machine it is effective on receipt. It is then that a legally binding contract will be recognised. This differs from the postal rule where an acceptance is complete on the posting.

21   B

Where a contract is of a social or domestic nature then the courts will assume no intention to be legally bound exists. Equally if a contract is of a business nature such an intention to be legally bound will be presumed. In both instances the presumptions at law can be rebutted by the parties.

22   D

Rescission is an equitable remedy under which the parties will be restored to the position they enjoyed before the contract was commenced. Any money and goods handed over must be returned where the order is made. The nature of the contract and forms of consideration can prevent rescission being possible.

23   A

A contract is created immediately an offer is accepted. The contract need not be in written form, and therefore equally no signature need be provided. On payment of the price the contract obligation is completed rather than established at law.

24   A

The party making the promise is prevented at Common Law from going back on the promise as the lesser amount of money is to be paid before the due date for payment under the original contract. The promise to accept the lesser payment is binding because of the new undertaking given by the other party. Estoppel does not apply as this merely serves to suspend an obligation rather than change permanently an obligation.

25   C

The innocent party does not have solely the remedy of rescission available to them. They can seek this equitable remedy or seek damages, but not both.

26   C

A breach of condition goes to the heart of a contract and enables the innocent party to treat the contract as at an end if they wish. A breach of warranty is the breach of a term that is peripheral or secondary to the main contract terms, and enables the innocent party to seek damages. The contract here, however, cannot be treated as at an end. The distinction between conditions and warranties is therefore important in relation to the remedies available not merely the amount of damages that might be awarded. Specific performance is an equitable remedy that can be sought on breach of condition. The innocent party, however, is not confined to seeking this remedy.

27   B

Once an agreement exists the obligations of both contracting parties can be identified. Failure to satisfy the requirements as identified amounts to breach of contract. The factor of reasonableness is irrelevant as the courts would look to the parties simply complying with obligations as identified. The contract will not be frustrated as this will only arise where performance becomes impossible or radically different from that anticipated.

28   D

A party having acted unfairly will have no implications on the contract. The courts simply look to whether or not the parties have complied with contractual requirements. Further, the courts will look to the remedy of damages being appropriate. It is only if damages will not be appropriate that the remedy of specific performance can be ordered.

29   A

The reply is a request for information and as such has no effect on the offer. It is when a counteroffer is made that the original offer is destroyed. On the facts the offer is accepted as required and so a legally binding contract would be recognised. Revocation of an offer by post is only effective when received.

30   C

A legally binding contract exists as £24 is sufficient consideration. The courts do not consider the actual value of the consideration provided in a contract. They merely look to enforcing the agreement of the parties. 'Adequacy' relates to monetary value, and consideration need not be adequate.

31   C

Frustration occurs when performance of a contractual obligation becomes impossible to perform or becomes radically different from that originally anticipated. The fact that performance will take longer and/or will become more expensive does not amount to performance being deemed radically different.

32   C

As the contract is under deed the time period applicable is 12 years. Under a simple contract the time limit is only 6 years.

33   D

A requirement for a legally binding contract is that both contracting parties provide consideration. Where only one party is to provide consideration, a gift rather than a contract is recognised, and a gift is not legally enforceable. If, however, an undertaking to provide consideration by one party alone is identified under a deed this will be legally binding.

34 **D**

In order for a legally binding contract to be recognised the offer must be accepted. The acceptance must be blanket and unequivocal. If the response to an offer identifies a change to a material factor, this will constitute a counter offer, which in turn has the effect of terminating the original offer.

35 **C**

The response to the offer introduces to the contract something new. It is not a blanket acceptance of that offered. It is a counteroffer and discharges the original offer.

36 **C**

Consideration need not be adequate. 'Adequacy' relates to monetary value and the courts will not consider this issue, but merely look to enforcing the agreement between the two parties. Both parties must provide consideration which must be sufficient in that it is something the courts recognise irrespective of its value. Contracting parties must provide consideration but not necessarily to each other.

37 **B**

On the facts past consideration is identified. A promise is provided that does not form consideration in return for that already done. That done is past consideration and cannot constitute good consideration in relation to a subsequent promise. Money is a significant factor under the contract so the contract would be regarded as legally binding, and registration would not be necessary.

38 **B**

A contract is a private agreement and only the parties to the agreement can sue. Other parties may have an interest in the contract obligations being performed but they do not have the right to bring proceedings.

39 **C**

A blanket acceptance is not provided. Nor is the response a request for information which would cause the offer to remain open. The response is a counteroffer and destroys the original offer.

40 **B**

Where goods are sold in the course of a business the implied condition applies. It is irrelevant whether the goods are sold to a consumer or not. This can be of significance with regard to the exclusion of liability for breach of the implied term.

41 **D**

Consideration must be sufficient. However, where a party is to do something that they are legally required to do anyway, this will not be deemed sufficient. It will not be illegal, nor will it be seen as past consideration as we are not looking to something done in the past but something required to be done in the future. Further, consideration need not be adequate.

THE LAW OF EMPLOYMENT

42   B

If a person is dismissed without justifiable reason they have a claim on the basis of unfair dismissal. Justifiable reasons do exist but these do not apply on the facts of the scenario. They include such grounds as lack of capability and if continued employment would contravene a statute.

43   A

No obligation attaches to employers to provide a reference. Where a reference is provided the employer must take care to ensure that information provided is correct. An implied duty does attach to employers to act reasonably and responsibly towards employees.

44   C

The law is specific in identifying the set time period within which an employee becomes entitled to particulars of his employment.

45   B

Trade union activity, pregnancy and complaints regarding health and safety matters are grounds upon which it is automatically unfair to dismiss an employee. However, for an employee to refuse to obey a reasonable instruction, an employer could fairly dismiss the individual. Such refusal could be seen as clear breach of contract.

46   C

Wrongful dismissal amounts to breach of contract on the part of the employer and the employee can pursue an action in the civil courts or at an employment tribunal. If the claim is successful, a basis for setting the limit of the financial liability exists. No statutory right to wrongfully dismiss a person exists. It is contradictory to suggest as such.

47   C

The Sex Discrimination Acts 1975 and 1986, the Race Relations Act 1976 and the Disability Discrimination Act 1995 are relevant in prohibiting discrimination in areas identified in A, B and D. Age discrimination is eliminated under the Employment Equality (Age) Regulations 2006, not an Act of Parliament.

48   B

Duties relate to the selection and training of staff. This includes a duty to dismiss where behaviour is dangerous. Duties relating to the provision of machinery and equipment exist. It is no defence for an employer to prove that he obtained equipment from a reliable supplier.

49   C

Six directives resulted in six Regulations being introduced dealing with employer responsibilities related to health and safety. These collectively served to replace the patchwork legislation that had previously been relevant.

COMPANY ADMINISTRATION

50   C

The articles of association constitute a contract binding on the members and company. Any alteration must therefore be for the company as a whole. The alteration must be for the benefit of the company, that is the corporators. The alteration need not be for the benefit of creditors, therefore A is incorrect. It is inappropriate to look to benefits of future members. Equally it is wrong to highlight the majority of members, even though circumstances in cases have resulted in varied interpretations of "the company as a whole". B and D are therefore also incorrect.

51   A

Unless the company decides otherwise, the quorum, or minimum number of persons required to be in attendance for the meeting to be valid and decisions made effective is two members or two who are the proxies for members.

52   A

A partnership is not a legal entity. The partners collectively are seen as the partnership with joint and several liability attaching as well as joint ownership of the partnership assets. A company has legal personality. Being a "legal person" it can own property, rather than ownership reside with the shareholders.

53   D

Articles of association are contractually binding on members and the company only. Where a director is also a member the court would consider the capacity relevant director/shareholder in relation to the relevant issue. Here the articles refer to disputes between the company and directors, so that is the capacity that would be recognised. The article would be seen as constituting a rule and not a contract term.

54   C

Where a company is limited by guarantee, the guarantors will identify the amount of their personal guarantees. An individual guarantor is only liable for the amount identified, not the full company indebtedness. Information of each guarantor's personal potential liability would be found in the statement of guarantee. It is only in the event of a winding-up that the guarantor will be required to make payment.

55   B

A veil of incorporation exists, whereby the company is recognised as distinct from its members. However, in some instances the veil will be lifted and corporate liability can attach to physical persons. If the number of members of a public company falls below two, then any remaining member is permitted six months in which to restore the membership to the minimum required. If this is not done then any one member will become personally liable for company debts arising after the six-month period.

56   D

A public company must have in its name the letters plc or 'Public Limited Company'. The minimum paid-up share capital figure is not £50,000. This is the minimum authorised share capital figure. Further, restrictions can be placed on the transfer of its shares and its shares need not be publicly for sale. Note that the majority of public companies are not quoted on the stock exchange.

57   B

A promoter is in a fiduciary position. Where a secret profit is achieved by a promoter, the company being promoted has the right to sue on the basis of breach of that fiduciary duty.

58   B

A conditional prohibition of the usage of certain words in a company name exists. Words that are misleading or give the wrong impression require approval for usage. The word "council" is suggestive of a local authority connection and so would require approval.

59   D

It is the subscribers alone who are required to sign the Memorandum of Association. The Memorandum must state that the subscribers agree to each take at least one share in the company. The requirement of signing the Memorandum, however, does not attach to people in these other capacities.

60   C

Prior to the Companies Act 2006 a maximum of fifteen months was allowed between Annual General Meetings being held. Now AGM's must be held within the 6 month period after the accounting reference date. The answer is therefore C.

61   D

Only an ordinary resolution is required to give directors authority to issue new shares. Any alteration to Articles of Association or a Memorandum of Association requires a special resolution.

62   A

Information of the share capital must be provided in the Memorandum of Association. The specific requirement is that the total authorised capital figure be stated.

63   A

The word "limited" relates to the fact that the financial liability of members is limited to the amount they have paid and/or agreed to pay for shares. Equally, if a person is a member of an unlimited company then the financial liability of the member is literally unlimited. This personal liability to satisfy the company debts would arise on a winding-up.

64   C

For a director to achieve a personal profit in a contract with the company, liability for breach of fiduciary duty can be identified. However, this is where the profit had not been disclosed. To retain a secret profit would be breach of fiduciary duty. However, if the profit is disclosed to the board, Popeye may keep the profit.

65   D

On formation of a company it is not necessary that articles of association be submitted to the Registrar of Companies. Where the document is not provided then the model form Table A articles will automatically apply. The company can then subsequently pass a special resolution in order to make changes to that model form as applicable to the company.

66   D

Sometimes the Companies Act 2006 does stipulate a minimum percentage of shareholders who can formally object to changes proposed by the majority. On a resolution to change a company name, no statutory right to object is provided.

67   D

A minimum 95% members support is needed for a plc to hold an AGM on shorter notice than that stipulated in legislation. A minimum 90% support is required in the case of a private company.

68   B

Where a party enters into a contract with a company, and the contract is not specifically permitted by the objects clause, the contract will nevertheless be binding. S40 provides that a company is not now restricted in its commercial dealings by that identified in its objects clause. At law a company can now enter into any lawful contract and so has absolute contractual capacity. The company can, however, impose limitations and prohibitions on this freedom of activity afforded by the law.

69   D

An ordinary resolution can be passed at general meeting with 50% + support. Prior to the Companies Act 2006 a written resolution usually needed unanimous support. The Act now permits a written ordinary resolution to be passed with the same support as needed at a meeting 50%+.

70   C

A special resolution can be passed at general meeting with a minimum 75% support. Prior to the Companies Act 2006 a written resolution usually needed unanimous support. The Act now permits a written special resolution to be passed with the same support as that required at a meeting 75%.

71   D

The Companies Act 2006 recognises the use of electronic communication as valid to a notable extent. Content takes account of communications to Companies House as well as members. The support required in order that the company can communicate with members through the use of electronic means can be approved either by members in general meeting or under the articles of association.

72   B

Under the Companies Act 2006 if information is provided electronically, that same information must be provided to members or debenture holders free of charge in hard copy form where requested.

73   C

Whilst it will be permissible to communicate electronically with members, approval at general meeting or under the articles of association must exist. No automatic right to communicate in this way is given.

COMPANY FINANCE AND MANAGEMENT

74   D

As the shareholders are the owners and controllers of the company, they have the power to appoint and remove directors. Equally they must, in general meeting, pass a resolution to approve any compensation payment for loss of office. The directors and creditors do not have this authority, and the inland revenue would not need to approve the payment.

75   B

If such a transaction is not approved by the company in general meeting it is not automatically void. It will in fact be valid unless it is avoided by the company. The director will have supported the transaction, they cannot therefore subsequently look to the transaction being avoided.

76   D

As the securities are identified as £1 shares, then this is the appropriate issue price. The price of shares quoted on the stock exchange can change and become higher or lower than the issue price.

77   D

Whilst a director is not an employee of the company, they can in addition be an employee, for example a finance director who is also a company accountant. A director can also be an independent contractor of the company. Shareholders can be employees of the company. This is shown with the many employee shareholder schemes that exist. A partner cannot be an employee of the firm. A partnership is not a legal entity and so employees are actually employed by the partners. A person cannot be an employer of himself.

78   B

Since 1992, one member private companies have been permitted. Such a member can also be the sole director of the company. Under the C.A. 2006 a private company no longer must appoint a company secretary.

79   B

The CA2006 provides that public companies cannot issue shares in return for work or services. A private company can issue shares paid up to any nominal value. A private company can have a share capital of any amount. Further, private companies can issue shares in return for consideration of any value. No valuation is necessary. Also, no blanket provision exists that shares cannot be issued at a discount to market value.

80   A

A floating charge attaches to a class of assets which can be disposed of by the company in the ordinary course of business. The assets within the class can, therefore, change from time to time. It is a fixed charge that would be created over land, with the relevant property being specifically identified.

81   A

Whilst the section requires directors to have regard to the interests of employees, the employees cannot bring an action on the basis of an alleged breach. As the shareholders are the controllers of the company, it is they who would have this right.

82   A

Where an insolvent company is allowed to continue trading the directors may be held liable for wrongful trading. In the event of insolvency the company should cease trading. In such a situation the directors can be held personally liable to contribute to the company assets. Wrongful trading is not a criminal offence and so a fine would not be appropriate.

83   A

The section provides protection to minority shareholders. It is therefore they that have the right to petition. Any one member can petition irrespective of the number of shares they hold.

84   A

A director owes duties primarily to the members. It is the members who can therefore waive a breach of duty owed to them. This would require the passing of a resolution at the general meeting.

85   B

An ordinary resolution with special notice is required to remove a director. A simple majority vote is required. The notice required is as for an ordinary resolution plus the special notice requirement which is a further 7 days. This type of resolution is little used, being appropriate only in relation to directors and auditors.

86   B

Shares can be issued in order to raise money for a building project. The other options identified do not show actions that would necessarily be in the best interests of the company.

87   D

The recognised definition of a floating charge provides that it attaches to a class of assets which can be present or future. Further, the company has the power to dispose of such assets in the ordinary course of business. D provides the fullest, and an accurate definition. Certain other options identified are not necessarily wrong, but lack relevant features.

88   D

Where directors are in breach of fiduciary duty but the conduct can be seen as going beyond this and amounting to fraud, then a minority action can be brought and be successful. The fraud need not be deliberate. The courts have interpreted fraud as being short of that required in the criminal sense.

89   A

Because a company is a "legal person", it can be a contracting party. Further, the company can sue and be sued. John has contracted with Lamb Ltd. Privity of contract applies and only these two parties can sue or be sued on the contract. A veil of incorporation exists, whereby Larry is recognised as being separate from the company.

90   C

Freedom of contractual ability for all charities is not permitted under the Act. Whilst companies are given absolute freedom of contractual ability, the company itself can impose restrictions and limitations on its activities. These must be identified in the company articles of association. Under the C.A. 2006 the articles become the dominant document.

91   D

Generally shares cannot be issued at a discount. They must be issued at value or at a premium. The issuing of shares at a discount is only possible in limited instances. A share premium account, made up of monies paid for shares beyond the value cannot be used to write off a discount relating to any other shares in the company.

92   C

A director has apparent authority to act on behalf of the company. Express authority is not needed. Where a person acts as managing director not having been appointed to that position, his actions will be binding. Certainly where the other directors are aware of the conduct and through omission allow it to continue, then the company will be bound by the actions of the individual.

93   C

Under s214 of the Insolvency Act 1986, it is only the directors who can be personally liable for wrongful trading. For liability to attach to all persons who took part in it would be far too wide. Further, whilst persons other than directors can be deemed officers for certain purposes, for example the company secretary, they cannot be liable under this section.

94   C

Pre the CA2006 legislation set out the procedure to be followed by a private company wishing to provide financial assistance for the acquisition of its own shares. No court approval was needed. However, needed was a special resolution, a statutory declaration provided by the directors and an auditors report. Under the CA2006 no authority is now needed so long as the company is not a subsidiary of a public company.

95   C

The legislation relates specifically to the allotment by the company of equity shares for cash.

96   D

Generally loans to directors were prohibited under the Companies Act 1985. The Companies Act 2006 introduced a change whereby on the facts member approval is needed. D is therefore the correct answer.

97   A

Where directors act beyond the power given to them the members have the power to ratify such conduct and relieve the directors from personal liability. A resolution on each issue passed by the members in general meeting would be required.

98   D

If a person disqualified from acting as a director nevertheless does so act they can incur personal liability for company debts. A winding-up does not of itself give rise to director personal liability. Equally, where a director is liable for fraudulent trading, criminal sanctions will apply. A director found liable for wrongful trading can be held liable to contribute to the company assets.

99   C

Private companies will not be required to appoint a company secretary whilst the need to appoint will still apply to public companies. A private company will be able to appoint to this position, in which case the same obligations would then apply.

100 B

A service address only will be on public record at Companies House. At present a director's home address is available from records. With implementation of the relevant CA2006 content the domestic address of directors will be on file but generally not accessible by the public.

ETHICS AND BUSINESS

101 C

100.2 of the CIMA Code of Ethics requires that "Professional accountants are required to apply this conceptual framework to identify threats to compliance with the fundamental principles, to evaluate their significance and, if such threats are other than clearly insignificant to apply safeguards to eliminate them or reduce them to an acceptable level such that compliance with the fundamental principles is not compromised." This is because the highest possible professional standards are expected and the safeguards provide practical and straightforward means by which most ethical problems can be easily addressed.

102 C

100.5 of the CIMA Code of Ethics explain that "a framework to assist a professional accountant to identify, evaluate and respond to threats to compliance with the fundamental principles." Rules tend to provide a means of identifying what should or should not be done, but provide little guidance on how to engage in ethical reasoning or problem-solving. You have either broken or not broken a rule, but life is seldom that clear-cut and rules cannot provide for every eventuality.

103 A

False: 130.6 of the Code of Ethics states that "where appropriate, a professional accountant should make clients, employers or other users of the professional services aware of limitations inherent in the services to avoid the misinterpretation of an expression of opinion as an assertion of fact".

B

False: 130.5 of the Code of Ethics states that "a professional accountant should take steps to ensure that those working under the professional accountant's authority in a professional capacity have appropriate training and supervision".

C

True: 130.4 of the Code of Ethics state that "diligence encompasses the responsibility to act in accordance with the requirements of an assignment, carefully, thoroughly and on a timely basis". Inevitably, diligence represents a balance between punctiliousness and punctuality!

104

Safeguards in the work environment include, but are not restricted to:

The employing organisation's systems of corporate oversight or other oversight structures.

The employing organisation's ethics and conduct programmes.

Recruitment procedures in the employing organisation, emphasising the importance of employing high calibre competent staff.

Strong internal controls.

Appropriate disciplinary processes.

Leadership that stresses the importance of ethical behaviour and the expectation that employees will act in an ethical manner.

Policies and procedures to implement and monitor the quality of employee performance.

Timely communication of the employing organisation's policies and procedures, including any changes to them, to all employees and appropriate training and education on such policies and procedures.

Policies and procedures to empower and encourage employees to communicate to senior levels within the employing organisation any ethical issues that

Safeguards created by the profession, legislation or regulation include, but are not restricted to:

Corporate governance regulations,

Code of Ethics.

Educational, training and experience requirements for entry into the profession.

External review by a legally empowered third party of the reports, returns, communications or information produced by a professional accountant.

Professional or regulatory monitoring and disciplinary procedures.

Continuing professional development requirements.

Professional standards.

Effective, well-publicised complaints systems operated by the employing organisation, the profession or a regulator, which enable colleagues, employers and members of the public to draw attention to unprofessional or unethical behaviour.

An explicitly stated duty to report breaches of ethical requirements.

105 A

is not really an ethical reason. Qualifications are important for career progression, partly because they do mark competence, but self-promotion is not an object of ethical behaviour, but a benefit of it;

B

is relevant, but not really in strict ethical terms. Qualifications do help with public confidence, but the ethical duty of accountants is to be forthright about their own abilities. You may pass an exam, but it does not mean that you really understand something in depth. The duty is to really understand your work and to continue to be better at it, rather than merely to have the piece of paper;

C

is highly relevant because the self-imposed obligation to develop is the only way in which CIMA can ensure that accounting standards are actually met in the current context. The problem that professional bodies face is that it takes longer to put in place new standards and training than is desirable. The accountant is under a continuing duty to actively look for ways in which to provide service that is appropriate to the needs of contemporary business and practice. This is as true of ethical standards as of accounting practice standards;

D

is relevant because causing financial loss to the client or to society is the antithesis of what accountants might wish to do. However, the financial impact of ethical behaviour is not the only consideration. Accountants need to be up to date in areas relating to professional conduct and practice that may not have an obvious or direct effect on financial transactions. The Code makes this quite clear;

E

is a laudable sentiment, but self-development is not actually the ethical motivation for the duty to improve and learn. The duty is to learn and improve in the interests of clients and society.

F

is indirectly relevant. Firms are under an ethical duty to make clear their capabilities and capabilities of their staff. Training and qualification frameworks are essential safeguards for ethical practice. However, the individuals responsibility to develop himself or herself is not because the boss wants to vaunt your qualifications, but because you should be and be seen to be competent to do your job in prevailing professional conditions.

106 **A**

Reliability is a specific virtue because of the importance of being diligent to the client in the delivery or service, to the profession in the maintenance of a positive reputation and to the public in the trust that can be placed in accountants' reports and assurances.

B

Accuracy is not explicitly stated as a virtue. Accuracy is obviously the product of diligent work and an essential quality in work, but is an outcome, rather than an attribute of a person. Ethical virtues are qualities of people, rather than of work;

C

Diversity awareness is not explicitly addressed by the Code. There are substantial legal duties on people to avoid discrimination in all aspects of life, but accountants are to behave objectively. The general duty of respect for all clients and so on covers respect, regardless of race, gender and so on;

D

Financial responsibility is not a specific object of the Code, since the ethical Code focuses on those circumstances that surround the preparation of work that might affect the reliability or weight of that work;

E

Social responsibility is at the heart of the Code because the accountant owes a duty to the public and society to ensure that financial matters are carried out in an honest and transparent way. In many respects, the development of modern accounting is driven by the need of society to faith in financial processes. Therefore, the accountant should be able to respond (be responsible) to that need;

F

Loyalty, while being a desirable quality in many ways, even reflected in duties of trust and confidence to the employer at law and to clients in terms of confidentiality is not explicitly a part of the Code. Loyalty may, in fact, give rise to ethical problems where loyalty to friends, colleagues, causes or family can conflict with social responsibility. Effectively, the accountant's ultimate responsibility is to the society;

G

Courtesy is specifically mentioned because it links in with respect and professionalism in dealing with clients. While it may seem less critical than some of the other virtues, clearly it is the springboard of other professional relationships, particularly trust, which is the underpinning principle upon which an accountant must base much of his or her work;

H

Fidelity or faithfulness is much the same as loyalty. While it might be generally socially desirable, the professional obligation to society can often mean that duties of fidelity are in conflict with broader public duties;

I

Punctuality is not explicitly said in those words. However, timeliness is. Different words can mean the same thing and the key to the Code is to understand the reasoning, rather than applying the strict letter of the 'law'. Timeliness is vitally important because it is linked to reliability, due diligence and care. No accountant needs reminding that time is money;

J

Respect is a key feature of the Code and underpins the trust needed to maintain professional relationships. If mutual respect is built up, it often makes addressing ethical problems considerably easier and avoids them altogether. It also has an impact on the perception of the profession by the public and the extent to which a firm can be seen to be complying with other social responsibilities like appreciating and responding to the diverse needs of clients.

107

All of these are potentially breaches of the principle of integrity. Even if information is freely available, it may not be clear that it is important in the context of the work undertaken. As such, the accountant may be misleading the client by leaving it to the client to find out something. Similarly, partial information may be highly misleading. Forgetting to mention important information, unless inadvertent, could be classed as being reckless. There is a duty to be careful that is bound up with the concept of integrity. Regardless of the duty of trust and confidence, the client should not be kept in the dark to avoid embarrassment. It may be in the latter circumstances, that some urgent consultations within the firm or with a regulator or legal advisers may be appropriate.

108 A

False: The duty of confidentiality extends even to social situations (140.2 of the CIMA Code).

B

False: The duty of confidence subsists for past, present and future clients (140.3 and 140.6 of the CIMA Code).

C

False: Know-how and skills learned from doing a task is transferable. What is not acceptable is passing on or using information, rather than learning from experience (140.6 of the CIMA Code).

109 C

is probably the most accurate statement, since the CIMA Code draws very heavily from the IFAC Code. There is an element of truth in D as well, since some aspects of the IFAC Code probably set the standards at a lesser level than UK Law and standards would accept. Neither of the first two statements are true. The approach used in both Codes is essentially the same.

110 C

is the correct answer. The Financial Reporting Council is an independent, non-governmental regulator which ensures that corporate bodies in general inspire public confidence because of sound financial reporting, but that it is independent from political interference. The Professional Oversight Body for Accounting can make recommendations for change, but cannot make new rules on its own account.

111 A

is not a Principle of Standards in Public Life. Transparency is important, but it is a quality of processes, not of individuals. The standards focus on the individual's own duty to make systems transparent.

Selflessness and Integrity highlight that self-interest and the vulnerability to outside influences should be avoided. Objectivity and Accountability emphasise the importance of decision-making based on facts and relevant considerations which can be justified with reference to clear reasoning and evidence.

Openness, Honesty and Leadership all are behaviours that require the individual to take on responsibility for what they do and they know and to actively follow the right course of action, engendering trust and confidence.

112 D

is correct. Corporate responsibility is not a question of alleviating the individual responsibility of professionals to act in a professional way, although a company should support, supervise and scrutinise the behaviour of its professional employees and bear responsibility when they fall short of the standards expected of them.

Neither does corporate responsibility mean that traditional business partners, in the sense of employees, clients and stakeholders are the only concern of a business. Nor should good Public Relations (PR) be confused with a sense of responsibility to the community. In many ways, Ethical Values and Corporate Responsibility Agendas will make for good PR, but that is not the motivating factor, nor should it be. Initiatives motivated by marketing, rather than principle are ultimately more likely to inspire cynicism than trust.

113 D

is correct. These are the three aspects that are personal, that is they are part of the behaviour and make-up of an individual, and they are qualities, states of mind or personal attributes, rather than attitudes.

114 B

is correct. Although a client might request the disclosure of information, there may be certain circumstances when that information might include other confidential information, relating to another party. However, when refusing to disclose, reasons should be given and a second opinion in principle might be sought from the person responsible for Information and Data compliance in your organisations. Requests from the regulator, unless they are acting unlawfully, will normally be appropriate to disclose information.

Requests made by solicitors, are not in themselves, requests where there is a legal obligation to disclose. The reason for the request should be a reason where there is a legal or professional obligation to disclose or where the person requesting the information through the solicitor is the sole subject of it. Solicitors' letters should be dealt with in a courteous and timely way, but should not be assumed to have any greater weight in themselves than a request by any other member of the public.

Requests by your employer, other than as part of regulatory review or because the matter is being dealt with by a variety of people across the office, all subject to the same confidentiality, should be treated with care and should fall in the category of acceptable disclosures within the terms of your Data and Information Management procedures. Most damaging breaches of confidentiality occur as a result of internal disclosure where the recipient is unaware of the confidential nature of the material they are receiving.

115

While there is considerable overlap, the following may be your first port of call in resolving the issues raised. In respect of the following problem situations, you would refer primarily to (A) the IFAC Code, (B) the CIMA Code, (C) the Law, (D) or apply professional judgement:

1   **C** A request to disclose data relating to a client to a non-accounting regulatory body, for example the Inland Revenue, probably raises the question of whether there is a specific legal duty to disclose. If the law requires you to assist a body such as the Inland Revenue, this overrides other obligations. Should you be unclear, you should consult CIMA for advice.

2   **A** A dispute over the proper returns relating to an off-shore company, if those relate to practices and activities in that jurisdiction would certainly be looked at in the light of the IFAC Code as a minimum. It may be that you feel that a higher level of ethical conduct is the responsible and professional course of action. Work undertaken in relation to the UK, even extra-territorially, should always be done with reference to the applicable domestic law and practice.

3   **D** Pressure being exerted as a result of a change of government policy on a the public sector client you are working for falls within both the Codes, but primarily is an issue of independence and integrity. Just because a client is operating public policy does not mean that specific actions might be in the public interest.

Examples such as local authority interest rate swaps in the 1980s and 1990s demonstrate that professional vigilance against public pressures as well as private interests are needed. However, this is largely a question of professional judgement.

4   **B** Disclosing information you have in your possession, that has not been actually requested, but might assist an investigation by CIMA into alleged ethical wrongdoing falls directly within the CIMA Code obligations.

ETHICAL CONFLICT

116

A   4   Preparing accounts for your spouse's business will clearly cause a personal conflict of interests.

B   5   In this situation the accountant would be reviewing, as auditor, the work that they had themselves completed which would hinder their independence.

C   1   Being a member of the campaign group, the accountant will be seen to be advocating the group.

D   3   Preparing accounts for someone that you are very familiar with can put pressure on the accountant to act favourably towards, in this situation, their relative.

E   2   Not wanting to lose their major client, the accountant may feel intimidated into meeting the deadline at the cost of the accuracy of their work.

117   A

True: 100.8 of the Code of Practice means that applying safeguards and remedying the problem is the core concern. It is easy to stray into the tricky ethical situations without noticing it. Ethical standards are about taking responsibility for choices, not punishing accountants who are the victims of circumstances.

B

False: 100.6 of the Code of Practice makes it clear that the accountant is responsible not only for what they know, but for what they can reasonably be expected to know. Inadvertent mistakes, by their nature, cannot be avoided. Problems that should be obvious to a well-trained, diligent accountant are their responsibility. 'I did not know' is no excuse if it would have been evident to any accountant.

C

True: 100.7 of the Code of Practice makes it clear that qualitative information should be taken into account. Sometimes the threats to ethics do not arise from accounting itself, but by surrounding circumstances.

D

True: 100.7 of the Code of Practice is pretty explicit about this. Obviously, an employer should have systems in place to allow people to apply safeguards in most situations and to maintain professional ethics. However, it is better to be unemployed than serving a prison sentence!

118   CLEARLY (D) IS THE RIGHT ANSWER.

You need to know what is happening first and work out whether there is an ethical issue arising. You then need to work out what sort of issue it is so you can use the guidance to determine how it ought to be dealt with according to professional standards. If internal mechanisms allow you to resolve it in accordance with professional standards, that is fine, but if there is a conflict between internal practice and the Code, then you may need to look for outside guidance. CIMA's ethics helpline would be a good start.

119   C

100.3 of the CIMA Code of Ethics "provides examples of safeguards that may be appropriate to address threats to compliance with the fundamental principles and also provides examples of situations where safeguards are not available to address the threats and consequently the activity or relationship creating the threats should be avoided". Because most frequent problems are anticipated by the Code and because it is drawn up in terms of values and principles, as well as specific rules, it is unlikely that there would be a threat not addressed in some way. However, accountants should not risk ethical misconduct, especially when dealing with new systems and business practices. Remember also that things can be lawful without being ethical!

120   C

The CIMA Code of Practice advises that (c) is the appropriate course of action: "100.20 If a significant conflict cannot be resolved, a professional accountant may wish to obtain professional advice from the relevant professional body or legal advisors, and thereby obtain guidance on ethical issues without breaching confidentiality."

121   A

True: 140.7 permits this (obviously where there are no other conflicting obligations).

B

True: 140.7 would suggest that this would be appropriate.

C

True: 140.7 requires compliance with technical, quality and regulatory obligations.

D

False: Unless there is a specific regulatory or professional duty, internal budgetary preparations would not, of themselves, justify disclosure.

E

False: A request from a solicitor does not necessarily amount to a legal or regulatory duty to disclose. Solicitors will sometimes ask for things that you could legally disclose, but where it would be not consistent with professional ethics to disclose.

122

Integrity – When you are asked to contact the client to tell them that there has been a problem with the system, (5) you are, in effect, being asked to tell a lie. At the very least you would be being reckless with the truth of having checked it if you sign it off without looking at it (7).

123

Objectivity – It may be a small inducement, but it is an inducement when Sima says there is a drink in it for you if you help (9). The fact that you and Sima are friends and so you want to help (8) might indicate that you are being influenced in your decision- making by familiarity.

124

Professional Competence and Due Care – When Sima says she has not been able to produce a promised report on time (2), it is clear that she is not professionally competent, which is reinforced by the fact that she is not able to operate the new software system that she has not got to grips with yet (3).

125

Confidentiality – Generally, you should not be party to more than you wish to know about the background to the client's request (6), but then there can be a duty to disclose to a regulatory body when she tells you not to tell anyone in case she gets into trouble (10).

126

Professional Behaviour – There is normally an appropriate way in which a complaint from a client (1) should be dealt with, while there is a continuing duty to develop, not only core skills, but those needed to work effectively for clients. Sima has compromised this when she could not make it to the training event (4).

127

The problem presents potential for a conflict of interest and a simple ethical dilemma.

A

Do you do what your boss wants, or do what is demanded by professional ethics. This is easily solved. Pleasing the boss is lower down the hierarchy of priorities and is not really part of the framework of accounting professional ethics;

B

A lot of people would resolve this in practice by a 'white lie'. The only thing is that you are not actually dealing with the problem and hardly in the spirit of openness and honesty. Besides, although you have not attended, it concedes that your barriers to ethical conduct are your personal convenience, rather than facing up to problems and resolving them;

C

Accepting the invitation may not be a problem if you have already weighed up the facts and decided there is no real potential for conflicting interests, but going and not giving the other client some indication of your intentions so to do may create more problems than it solves. Secrecy, which is the opposite of openness, tends to fuel suspicions;

D

Is the correct answer. Looking at the facts and determining first whether there is an ethical issue is the necessary first step. After that, if there is potential for a conflict of interest, then you should say so to the boss and refuse. If the boss insists, then you might wish to try and resolve it using a third party in the firm. If there is no potential for conflict, it may nonetheless be advisable to check with both clients that they have no objection to ensure that they do not perceive there to be a conflict.

E

Displacing the problem by getting the client to make the decision for you is not managing the problem. Moreover, it may be in one client's perceived interest for you to attend. Conflicts of interest tend to favour one party practically more than the other.

128 A

Generally speaking a guess is a falsification and this is dishonest.

B

Ignoring the problem simply short-changes your employer, which is depriving the employer of fees to which they would have been entitled, had you done your job properly.

C

Maintaining the trust of the client in the firm and the profession is important and, although at some point it may be necessary to inform the client, if you plan to bill them after all, then it is most appropriate for you to use the internal processes first.

D

Unfortunately, we have to face the consequences of our mistakes. There is almost certainly a procedure in the company either for writing off these errors or for communicating and negotiating with clients. However, if your boss simply tells you to falsify it, then this does not absolve you of your ethical responsibility to do the right thing. You may wish to seek alternative advice from another manager or from your audit committee.

129 A

CIMA is always a useful source of advice and guidance, although using your internal processes first may give you a specific local resolution;

B

Board of your Organisation can provide guidance and will ultimately have to take responsibility for the wrongdoings of employees;

C

Audit Committee of your Organisation are there to ensure that care and standards are met. Normally the audit committee will comprise people with considerable experience and expertise in dealing with problems in an effective and professional way;

D

Legal and Compliance Department will often be a good port of call, although there may be a tendency to look at what the rules require, rather than what is ethical best practice;

E

Your solicitors are your affair. If you are worried about your own status, then taking legal advice is sensible, but it would be inappropriate to seek professional guidance on an ethics matter from them;

F

Your line-manager is normally the first port of call, unless he is part of the problem. While a manager cannot relieve you of your personal professional responsibilities for ethical decision-making, they may be able to help shoulder the burden or help you see the problem in a less alarming light.

130 A

Your line-manager is normally the first port of call, unless he is part of the problem. While a manager cannot relieve you of your personal professional responsibilities for ethical decision-making, they may be able to help shoulder the burden or help you see the problem in a less alarming light. However, you need to be aware of all of the facts first.

B

It is assumed that you have read, learned and inwardly digested the CIMA Code of Practice, although revisiting it to check that what you consider is an issue, actually is an ethical problem after you have . . .

C

. . . properly checked your facts. Careful analysis of what is really going on will often reveal that the ethical problem is less difficult than it seems. People often panic when faced with ethical problems and often they will disguise as a dilemma a situation where this only one right course of action, but is simply quite unpalatable. Most 'ethical dilemmas' are confused priorities, e.g. do I please the boss or look after the client's best interests. Most potential conflicts of interests are when there is a really tempting opportunity and you want to have your cake and eat it. Most ethical mistakes cause real problems because people try to hide their mistake and try to undo things for themselves, rather than owning up and seeking help.

D

Most people struggle with ethical problems. Often the people who have been around the longest with the quick 'pragmatic' solution are not actually thinking about the problem at all. Take advice, but always check your facts, check to see whether what you have in front of you is a real ethical issue, seek guidance from the Code and the firms procedure and use the mechanisms in place in the firm and beyond to face the problem and resolve it.

CORPORATE GOVERNANCE

131 C

Fiduciary duties are relevant to the area of corporate governance and the conduct of directors. However, corporate governance is primarily concerned with matters on a broader scale related to the company and company activity, such as overall control and accountability.

132 C

The fiduciary duties owed by officers of a company were established long before the creation of the European Union and before the establishing of any Codes relating to director conduct. The Courts of Equity served to develop and expand upon the Common Law. Fiduciary duties are an example of the role played by the Courts of Equity in developing the law.

133 B

Information of corporate borrowing was withheld. In order to achieve this, subsidiaries were formed. However, it was not this factor that was kept secret.

134 A

It was not felt necessary for a separate Code dealing with corporate governance in Europe be created. A need for a common approach was acknowledged, but it was felt that this could be achieved through the use of directives requiring individual member states to introduce laws.

135 B

The forum was set up acknowledging the need to further the development of a common approach within the EU. The forum is made up of 15 members.

136 A

It was the Cadbury Committee Report that contained this recommendation. This committee reported in 1992 and preceded the other committees/reports listed. Subsequent reports did address the question of executive director service contracts length, suggesting a shorter time period be appropriate.

Section 5

MOCK ASSESSMENT

1 **Which *one* of the following is *correct?***

  A   The House of Lords* has a discretion in applying English Law or European Law

  B   The House of Lords* must apply European Law where it contradicts English Law

  C   The House of Lords* can apply English Law even if it contradicts European Law

  D   The House of Lords* must obtain approval to apply European Law where it contradicts English Law

  *now Supreme Court

2 **Which *one* of the following courts has *no* criminal jurisdiction?**

  A   Divisional court of the Queens Bench Division

  B   County Court

  C   Magistrates Court

  D   Crown Court

3 **With judicial precedent, subject to the hierarchy of the courts, previous court decisions should be followed. However, it can be possible to avoid following precedent. Which *one* of the following is *incorrect* in relation to avoidance of precedent?**

  A   A higher court can overrule a lower court decision

  B   Any court can distinguish the facts from those of an earlier decision

  C   Any court can reverse the decision of a previous court

  D   Any court need not apply an *obiter dicta* statement of an earlier court

4 **In relation to establishing a claim of negligence, which one of the following is incorrect?**

  A   There must be sufficient proximity between the wrongdoer and the injured party

  B   The standard of care required is that expected by the reasonable person

  C   The same level of care is owed both to adults and children

  D   The level of care to be shown varies with the level of seriousness of the likely consequences of breach of duty

5 **Which *one* of the following is *correct?***

A   A professional adviser can be liable to both the client who employs them and any other parties who they know will rely on information provided

B   A professional adviser can be liable to anyone who relies on information they provide

C   A professional adviser will be liable in negligence but not contract for any negligent advice provided

D   A professional adviser cannot be liable where the only form of damage resulting from negligent advice given is financial loss

6 **The standard of proof to be satisfied in**

(i)   criminal actions

(ii) civil action is

A   Beyond reasonable doubt for (i) and (ii)

B   On a balance of probabilities for (i) and (ii)

C   Beyond reasonable doubt for (i) and on a balance of probabilities for (ii)

D   On a balance of probabilities for (i) and beyond reasonable doubt for (ii)

7 **Common Law developed from which one of the following?**

A   Equity

B   Custom

C   Decisions of the Court of Chancery

D   Judicial precedent

8 **Where a dispute involves issues of European Law the matter must be referred to the European Court by which of the following English courts?**

A   All

B   All the courts below the House of Lords*

C   Only the House of Lords*

D   Only the Court of Appeal and the House of Lords*

*now Supreme Court

9 **Which one of the following contracts would not be presumed to be legally binding?**

A   One or both contracting parties were a business or company

B   The contract was a collective agreement between employers and trade unions relating to terms of employment

C   The contract is of a clearly commercial nature

D   The contract involved money and this was a factor of significance

10 In which one of the following instances will misrepresentation generally not be recognised?

    A   The contract contains half-truths

    B   In a contract of the utmost good faith full disclosure is not made

    C   Information ceases to be accurate because of changed circumstances

    D   A party fails to disclose material facts

11 In which one of the following instances will a term not be incorporated into a contract?

    A   Where a party signs the contract containing the term, whether they have read it or not

    B   Where the term is an exclusion clause implied under the Unfair Contract Terms Act 1977

    C   Where there is a course of dealing between the parties

    D   Where reasonable notice of the term is given but a contracting party remains unaware of its existence

12 Liability in contract can never be excluded for which one of the following?

    A   Death or physical injury

    B   The implied conditions under the Sale of Goods Act 1979

    C   Financial loss

    D   Guarantees of goods given by manufacturers

13 The following advertisement appeared in a farming magazine. 'Plough for sale. Little used, very good condition £1000'. How would this statement be defined at law?

    A   Advertising puff

    B   Offer to sell

    C   Invitation to treat

    D   Invitation to buy

14 An offer was made by A to sell goods on the 1st April for £2,000. B the offeree telephoned A on the 5th April offering to pay £1,800 for the goods. On the 8th April, A offered to sell the goods to C for £1,900, and C accepted this offer on the same day. On the 7th April, B sent a letter to A which was received on the 10th April agreeing to pay the £2,000 asking price for the goods.

    A   There is a contract between A and B created on the 7th April

    B   There is a contract between A and B created on the 10th April

    C   There is a contract between A and C

    D   There is no contract created

15 **A coat was displayed in a shop window with a price tag attached which read £10. The price tag should have read £100. X who saw this went into the shop and demanded the coat for £10. Which one of the following is correct?**

A   As the window display is an offer X can demand the coat at £10

B   The window display is merely an invitation to treat and the shopkeeper does not have to sell the coat to X

C   The shopkeeper can refuse to sell the coat for £10, but cannot refuse to sell the coat to X for £100 if X was prepared to pay this sum

D   The shopkeeper would be bound to sell the coat to any customer prepared to pay this £100

16 **Which *one* of the following is *incorrect?***

A   A contract term can be implied by a court on the ground of business efficacy

B   A contract term can be implied by statute

C   A contract term can be implied by a court on the basis of fairness between the parties

D   A contract term can be implied by a court on the basic of trade custom

17 **Which one of the following statements is incorrect?**

A   Statute provides an implied term in sale of goods contracts that the goods are of satisfactory quality

B   Statute provides an implied term in sale of goods contracts that the goods supplied must correspond with description

C   Statute provides that failure to supply goods of satisfactory quality in a sale of goods contract constitutes breach of condition

D   Statute provides that failure to provide goods in a sale of goods contract that correspond with description amounts to a breach of warranty

18 **Which *one* of the following statements is *correct?***

A   In contract breach of a condition will result in the contract being terminated

B   In contract a breach of a condition is a breach of a term of fundamental importance to the contract

C   In contract a breach of warranty entices the innocent party to terminate the contract

D   In contract a breach of warranty can terminate a contract, but only on the basis of equity

19 Which *one* of the following is *incorrect?*

A   Exclusion clauses attempting to exclude liability for death or injury are void

B   Statutory implied conditions giving consumers protection in sale of goods contracts can be excluded so long as the exclusion clause is reasonable

C   Where the wording of an exclusion clause is ambiguous it will be interpreted against the party seeking to rely on it

D   An unfair term does not bind a consumer but the contract may continue

20 A contract will be discharged as a result of a frustrating event occurring. Which one of the following will not bring about discharge of a contract?

A   Performance becomes radically different from that anticipated

B   Performance becomes more expensive and difficult than anticipated

C   Physical impossibility of performance due to accidental destruction of subject matter

D   If the contract is dependent on a future event which does not occur

21 X has contracted with Y to paint a portrait of Y's daughter. Y has for a considerable time wanted X to paint the portrait and is very disappointed when X having started the work states that he is not prepared to complete the painting.

Which of the following remedies is appropriate in these circumstances?

A   Damages

B   Rescission

C   Specific performance

D   Injunction

22 Which of the following statements is *incorrect* in relation to the determining of damages payable on breach of contract?

A   The purpose of providing damages is to compensate the injured party

B   Quantifying damages is determining the actual amount of the award to be made to the injured party

C   The remoteness of damage issue is determined by considering the amount of damages the injured party reasonably expects on the basis of the contract breach and damages suffered

D   An innocent party has a duty to mitigate their loss

23 An employer must provide a written statement of particulars to an employee within what period from the commencement of the employment?

A   Immediately

B   Within 1 week

C   Within 1 month

D   Within 2 months

24   **In order to determine whether or not a party is an employee or an independent contractor a number of tests have been devised.**

Which one of the following is not a recognised test?

A   Organisation test

B   Control test

C   Multiple test

D   Supply and demand test

25   **Which *one* of the following statements is *incorrect?***

A   An employer is normally liable for wrongs committed by employees

B   An independent contractor has no statutory protection in respect of sick pay

C   An independent contractor has no preferential rights over other creditors on the insolvency of the employer

D   Employees and independent contractors are prohibited from delegating work to others

26   **Which one of the following is incorrect?**

A   A limited liability partnership has legal personality

B   A minimum two parties are required to form a limited liability partnership

C   Partners in a limited liability partnership cannot be corporate bodies

D   Individual members of a limited liability partnership will have no contractual liability to creditors of the partnership

27   **In relation to a private limited company, which one of the following is correct?**

A   Annual General Meetings must be held

B   Articles of Association must be filed with a Registrar when seeking registration of the company

C   The company will have perpetual succession

D   Directors of the company would never be liable to company creditors

28   **Which *one* of the following statements is *incorrect* in relation to a public limited company?**

A   A company must have a minimum issued share capital of £50,000

B   The company cannot issue only redeemable shares

C   The company must have a certificate of incorporation and a trading certificate before it can validly commence business

D   The company must have at least two members

29   Which *one* of the following is *incorrect?*

    A   Members of a company can ratify any *ultra vires* act of its directors

    B   Under the CA2006 the objects clause of an existing company will become a provision of its articles

    C   Where an objects clause provides that a company can carry on business as a 'general commercial company', the company can validly carry out any lawful transaction

    D   Where a director acts ultra vires on behalf of a company the transaction will be void unless it is ratified by the members

30   Which one of the following is correct in relation to an alteration of articles of association where the appropriate procedure is followed?

    A   Class rights can be altered

    B   Shareholder liability can be increased

    C   Members must pass an extraordinary resolution

    D   The alteration must be *bona fide* and in the best interests of every member

31   Which *one* of the following can only be achieved by a public limited company with court approval, in addition to a resolution of the members being passed?

    A   Change of company name

    B   Increase of share capital

    C   Reduction of share capital

    D   Change of the situation of the company registered office

32   Which one of the following is correct?

    A   A private company can issue only redeemable shares

    B   A private and a public company can issue only redeemable shares

    C   A public company can issue redeemable preference shares

    D   A private company cannot issue redeemable preference shares

33   One of the procedural requirements for the reduction of capital by a private limited company is the passing of a resolution.

    Which *one* of the following resolutions must be passed?

    A   Special

    B   Elective

    C   Written

    D   Ordinary

34   Which one of the following is incorrect?

A   A private company can accept any form of consideration in return for shares so long as it is real

B   A private company can accept consideration in a contract of allotment of shares of a lower value than that of the shares

C   A public company can only accept money as consideration on an allotment of shares

D   A private company and public company can increase its authorised share capital figure by passing a resolution

35   Where company articles do not identify a specific type of resolution appropriate, a company can increase its share capital if the members pass which *one* of the following types of resolution?

A   Ordinary

B   Special

C   Extraordinary

D   Special with extra notice

36   In relation to a company purchasing its own shares, which *one* of the following is *correct*?

A   Capital can be used by both private and public companies

B   Capital cannot be used by either private or public companies

C   Public companies only can use capital to satisfy some of the debt

D   Private companies only can use capital to satisfy some of the debt

37   In relation to a company providing financial assistance for the acquisition of its own shares, which *one* of the following is *incorrect*?

A   A private company may provide financial assistance for the purchase of its own shares

B   A public company can give financial assistance where it is given in good faith and is an incidental part of some larger purpose

C   A bank is permitted to provide financial assistance for an acquisition of shares in the bank itself

D   A company can provide assistance to employees by providing loans which are used to purchase shares in the company

38   Which *one* of the following statements is *incorrect*?

A   A private company can have only one member who is also the only director

B   A sole director in a private company can also be the company secretary

C   A sole member is distinct from the company at law

D   A director who is also sole shareholder in the company can waive their own breach of duty

39 A minority of members can give written, signed notice to the directors requiring them to hold a General Meeting.

Which *one* of the following is the *correct* minimum shareholding this minority must have?

A   5 per cent

B   10 per cent

C   15 per cent

D   25 per cent

40 Which *one* of the following is *correct in* relation to the use of an ordinary resolution with special notice?

A   It will only be used for the removal of a director

B   It will only be used for the removal of directors or auditors

C   It will only be used for the removal of directors and appointment of directors aged over 70 years

D   It will be used for the removal of directors and auditors, and also the appointment of a new director on a director removal and a new auditor appointment

41 In relation to directors which one of the following statements is incorrect?

A   A director is an agent of the company

B   A director is an officer of the company

C   A company has a duty to have executive directors

D   A shadow director is the main type of *de facto* director

42 Directors do not owe a duty to which *one* of the following?

A   Members individually

B   Members as a body

C   Creditors

D   Employees

43 Where a director is guilty of wrongful trading which one of the following is a possible consequence for the individual?

A   Being required to contribute to the assets of the company in liquidation

B   A possible fine

C   Imprisonment

D   Being subject to an equitable remedy

44 Which *one* of the following is *incorrect* where a director is in breach of fiduciary duty?

    A   The members can pass a resolution ratifying what has been done

    B   If the director in breach is also a member, he can vote in support of the ratification

    C   Articles can exempt directors from liability for breach of duty

    D   A director in breach can be liable to account for any secret profit obtained

45 Alan, Barbara and Clive are the only members of Beeceedee Ltd. with equal shareholdings. They are also the only directors of the company. Relations between the three parties have in the past been good. However, now, Alan and Barbara always vote against Clive at board meetings and are not prepared to listen to Clive's views. Further, on numerous occasions Alan and Barbara have refused to attend meetings. The quorum for board meetings and members meetings is two. Clive is unhappy generally with the way in which the company is now being run and wishes to petition for a winding up order.

Which *one* of the following is the appropriate action to obtain a winding up order?

    A   A derivative action

    B   An action on the basis of unfairly prejudicial conduct

    C   An action on the just and equitable ground

    D   A representative action

46 S996 CA2006 identifies a number of remedies which can be introduced by a court where an action for unfairly prejudicial conduct is brought. Which *one* of the following is *not* a remedy identified in this section?

    A   An order regulating company affairs in the future

    B   Authorising criminal proceedings to be brought in the name of and on behalf of the company

    C   Authorising civil proceedings to be brought in the name of and on behalf of the company

    D   Requiring the company to buy the petitioner's shares at fair value

47 Which one of the following is incorrect in relation to the company secretary?

    A   They can never contract on behalf of the company

    B   Qualification requirements attach to a company secretary of a public company but not a private company

    C   Details of the company secretary are not entered in the same register as that used to register director details

    D   A private company is not required to have a company secretary

48 Corporate governance measures are primarily for the benefit of 'stakeholders'. What are stakeholders in this context?

  A   All those directly or indirectly affected by the company's activities

  B   All those directly affected by the company's activities

  C   The shareholders

  D   All those indirectly affected by the company's activities

49 To which type of company is the Combined Code primarily directed?

  A   All companies

  B   All public companies

  C   All private and public companies

  D   All listed public companies

50 Which of the following is not a recommendation of the Combined Code?

  A   A board audit committee should be established

  B   The roles of Chairman and Managing Director should be combined

  C   At least one-half of the board should be made up of independent non-executive directors

  D   All directors should attend the AGM

51 The two-tier board structure comprises a Supervisory Board and what other organ?

  A   A board representing the employees

  B   A board majority of non-executive directors

  C   An all-executive board

  D   A management board

52 What is the most commonly used procedure adopted by the European Union for the creation of law?

  A   Consultation

  B   Codecision

  C   Assent

  D   Accord

53 The European Union is at present made up of how many states?

  A   18

  B   22

  C   27

  D   28

54 **In which one of the following countries are individuals appointed judges at the beginning of their legal careers?**

A   Germany

B   France

C   Denmark

D   Italy

55 **In the United States of America, all states with one exception have a common law system with court decisions establishing precedent. Which state is the exception?**

A   Ohio

B   Missouri

C   Louisiana

D   Texas

56 **Hong Kong and Macau on transferring sovereignty to China did not change their legal systems. They continue to adopt the legal systems of England and which other country?**

A   Australia

B   France

C   Spain

D   Portugal

57 **Which of the following is not an accurate description of what a company's code of ethics is likely to achieve?**

A   It tells employees what is expected of them in terms of behaviour

B   It explains the approach and outlook of the organisation

C   It encourages employees to take a consistent approach to ethical issues

D   It eliminates the need for legislation

58 **In which country does legislation legally require professional accountants to speak up if they find themselves in a situation where they might not be able to comply with relevant legal, regulatory or standards frameworks?**

A   Italy

B   USA

C   Germany

D   Japan

59 Which of the following actions by a company would not encourage employees to speak up if they encounter potentially serious cases of unprofessional or unethical behavior?

A   Introduce an employee helpline for ethics-related queries

B   State in the company's code of ethics that employees have a duty to speak up

C   Stress the importance of employees working together to meet ambitious sales targets

D   Develop a culture where it is safe and acceptable for employees to raise concerns

60 Which of the following is not an ethical value?

A   Tolerance

B   Truthfulness

C   Training

D   Transparency

61 Which of the following does not specifically relate to business ethics?

A   The financial viability of a business

B   The behaviour of the business and its employees

C   How a business conducts its relationships with its stakeholders

D   How a company does business, rather than what it does

62 Which of the following is not one of the five personal qualities that CIMA expects of its members?

A   Reliability

B   Respect

C   Responsibility

D   Reflection

63 While reviewing the work of one of your colleagues, you discover that he has made some extremely serious mistakes. When you discuss this with him, it becomes clear that he does not have the understanding of financial matters that he requires to be a competent accountant. This violates CIMA's fundamental principle of:

A   Integrity

B   Objectivity

C   Professional competence and due care

D   Confidentiality

64 You are working abroad and find yourself in a situation where a particular element of the country's legislation is in conflict with the IFAC Code of Ethics. In this situation you should:

    A   Obey the law because it is mandatory to comply with legislation

    B   Obey the ethics code because it is internationally binding

    C   Obey the law because you have a public duty to uphold the law, but not to uphold ethics

    D   Obey the ethics code because it is a requirement of your profession

65 Which of the following relates specifically to accountability?

    A   Taking responsibility for one's work and conclusions

    B   Maintaining clear records that provide evidence to back up conclusions

    C   Being answerable to queries in relation to one's work

    D   All of the above

66 Which of the following relates to an ethical issue?

    A   Moving into a larger office as part of a plan to expand your business

    B   Introducing a new monthly reporting process to maximise efficiency

    C   Introducing a new IT system to ensure confidentiality of customer information

    D   Recruiting a new finance director

67 Which of the following would be the least help in developing an effective corporate ethics programme?

    A   Having a chairman and chief executive who champion ethics at every opportunity

    B   Providing copies of the company's code of ethics to trusted personnel only to avoid the document falling into the hands of competitors

    C   Incorporating ethical issues into new employee induction programmes

    D   Talking to the company's key stakeholders about the social and environmental issues they believe to be important

68 In tackling ethical dilemmas, which of the following would not help you to find a solution?

    A   Establishing the facts and the ethical issues involved

    B   Referring to the CIMA and/or your company's code of ethics

    C   Following an established internal procedure

    D   Choosing to postpone tackling the issue due to pressure of deadlines

69   One of your colleagues has just been passed over for promotion for the third time. She shows you evidence that only a small number of women have ever been promoted to positions of seniority within your company. This, she says, is an issue of:

   A   Harassment

   B   Discrimination

   C   Conflict of interest

   D   Bribery and corruption

70   Which of the following is not an ethical issue for a bank?

   A   Providing accurate information about terms and conditions when advertising interest rates for customer loans

   B   Launching a premium account service for customers who are willing to pay a monthly charge for improved service

   C   Money laundering

   D   Disabled access to bank branches

71   Which of the following ethical issues is most likely to be affected by new developments in information technology?

   A   Data protection

   B   Gifts and hospitality

   C   Harassment

   D   Health and safety

72   Parliament has delegated wide powers to government ministers within their own departments. These ministers and their civil service departments are given the task of making rules and regulations within the guidelines of the enabling Acts. What is the usual form of these rules and regulations?

   A   Bye-laws

   B   Legislative Instruments

   C   Orders in Council

   D   Statutory Instruments

73   There are several sources of European Union Law. Which of the following are directly applicable and automatically become law in member states?

   A   Treaties only

   B   Treaties and Regulations only

   C   Treaties, Regulations and Directives only

   D   Treaties, Regulations, Directives and Decisions

74   **In contract law a misrepresentation is which *one* of the following?**

A   An untrue statement of fact or opinion which induces another to contract

B   An untrue statement of fact, opinion or intention which induces another to contract

C   An untrue statement of fact which induces another to contract

D   An untrue statement of fact or intention which induces another to contract

75   **Which of the following would *not* be a useful test for an ethical dilemma? Imagine how you would feel if your decision was splashed across the front pages of a newspaper?**

A   Whether your family would think what you have done is fair to everyone concerned?

B   Whether your decision would make you more popular in the office?

C   Whether you think you will be able to live with your decision?

D   Whether you think you will be able to live with your decision?

Section 6

ANSWERS TO MOCK ASSESSMENT

1	B	18	B	35	A
2	B	19	B	36	D
3	C	20	B	37	A
4	C	21	C	38	B
5	A	22	C	39	B
6	C	23	D	40	D
7	B	24	D	41	C
8	C	25	D	42	A
9	B	26	C	43	A
10	D	27	C	44	C
11	B	28	A	45	C
12	A	29	D	46	B
13	C	30	A	47	A
14	C	31	C	48	A
15	B	32	C	49	D
16	C	33	A	50	B
17	D	34	C	51	D

52	B	72	D
53	C	73	B
54	B	74	C
55	C	75	C
56	D		
57	D		
58	B		
59	C		
60	C		
61	A		
62	D		
63	C		
64	A		
65	D		
66	C		
67	B		
68	D		
69	B		
70	B		
71	A